Josef Herbasch

—

The Habad Movement in Israel

The Habad Movement in Israel

Religious Arguments in Politics

von
Josef Herbasch

Traugott Bautz
Nordhausen 2014

Bibliografische Information der Deutschen Bibliothek
Die Deutsche Bibliothek verzeichnet diese Publikation
in Der Deutschen Nationalbibliographie;
detaillierte bibliografische Daten sind im Internet
über http://dnb.ddb.de abrufbar.

Umschlagsentwurf von Hamid Reza Yousefi und Markus Rhode
Verlag Traugott Bautz GmbH
99734 Nordhausen 2014
Printed in Germany
ISBN 978-388-309-870-8
www.bautz.de

Inhaltsübersicht

Vorwort 7

Introduction 13

Chapter I:
Definition of Ultra-Orthodoxy 17

    1. Haredim 17
    2. History of Mitnaggdim 28
    3. History and Theology of Hasidism 32
    4. The Habad movement in its History and Theology 42
    5. Excursus: Messianism 49

Chapter II:
Habad in the State of Israel 53

    1. 'Who is a Jew?'-Debate 53
    2. Six Day War 72

Chapter III:
The settlement policy of the Habad movement and a comparison between the Habad movement and Gush Emunim 85

    1. Common Overview of the Settlement Policy 85
    2. Gush Emunim 93
    3. The Habad movement and its Approach to Settlement Policy ... 109

Chapter IV:
Conclusion 123

Chapter V:
Glossary 127

Chapter IV:
Bibliography 130

Vorwort

Das Verhältnis von Religion und Politik ist in den letzten Jahren wieder in der politisch-philosophischen Debatte mit der Aufmerksamkeit bedacht worden, die es verdient. Damit eröffnet sich zu Beginn des 21. Jahrhunderts ein interkulturelles Problemfeld, das in der Legitimatorik von Politik seit jeher eine zentrale Rolle spielt. Die Geschichte der Säkularisierung erweist sich, wie Charles Taylor gezeigt hat, keineswegs als jener lineare Weg, der in der Welt des ‚okzidentalen Rationalismus' behauptet worden ist. Nicht ohne Grund kamen wichtige Theoretiker der politischen Philosophie von Habermas über Derrida bis zu Agamben wieder auf das politisch-religiöse Problem zu sprechen, das in der zweiten Hälfte des 20. Jahrhunderts etwa bei Eric Voegelin oder Leos Strauss zum Schlüsselkonzept erhoben worden war.

Doch kaum werden diese Fragen auch in einem interkulturellen Blick verhandelt. Dies scheint aber unerlässlich, wenn man in die Differenz- und Konfliktstrukturen, aber unter Umständen auch das Ausgleichspotential säkularer und heiß religiöser Konzeptionen Einblick gewinnen will. Es gibt Regionen, in denen Religion und Politik kaum voneinander zu trennen sind. Dazu gehört unstrittig der Staat Israel, der von ultraorthodoxen Juden aus Prinzip abgelehnt wird. Das innere Spannungsfeld, das von gleichermaßen entscheidender Bedeutung für das Verhältnis von Religion und Politik und für die interkulturelle Philosophie ist, wird in Israel und den USA seit langem auf hohem Niveau diskutiert. In Deutschland findet man dazu kaum Veröffentlichungen. Die vorliegende kundige und umsichtige Studie von Josef Herbasch, ursprünglich eine von Professor Karsten Fischer betreute Magisterarbeit an der Ludwig Maximilian-Universität München, löst in spannender und intelligenter Weise dieses Desiderat ein.

Sowohl im politisch-philosophischen wie im interkulturellen Zusammenhang kommt dieser Studie eine Schlüsselbedeutung zu. Sie widmet sich Geschichte und Grundlage des ultraorthodoxen Judentums und der Rolle, die es im gegenwärtigen Israel spielt. Im Einzelnen stellt sich Herbasch die Frage, weshalb die Chabad-Bewegung so großes Interesse an der israelischen Politik nimmt, da sie doch dezidiert antizionistisch orientiert ist. Verfasser und Thema haben hier in idealer Weise zusammengefunden. Herbasch ist nämlich einerseits sehr gut bewandert in den theologischen und philosophischen komplexen Prinzipien des Chabad-Chassidismus. So hat er sich intensiv mit der Religionsphilosophie des Judentums und den Spannungen von Religion und Vernunft befasst. Zugleich ist er ein hervorragender Kenner der israelischen Innen- und Außenpolitik der vergangenen fünf Jahrzehnte und der einschlägigen Forschungen. Er ist auch mit der Scientific community in erstaunlicher Weise vernetzt.

Chabad ist eine ultraorthodoxe Bewegung. Unter den Ultraorthodoxen zeigt sie aber eine vergleichsweise große Offenheit und Diskussionsbereitschaft. Viele Debattenlinien laufen also in der Chabad-Bewegung zusammen. Einzelne dieser Problemknotenpunkte werden von Herbasch untersucht: so die Frage, wer überhaupt ein Jude ist, die Frage nach den theologischen Entwicklungen der Landnahme und der Siedlungen im Blick auf die messianische Erwartung.

Herbasch verbindet die verschiedenen Überlegungs- und Disziplinstränge souverän mit einander. Er beginnt im ersten Kapitel mit einer Definition der ‚Ultraorthodoxen‘. Dabei weist er darauf hin, dass ‚ultraorthodox‘ oder auch ‚Haredim‘ keine Selbstbezeichnung ist. Dafür wählt jene Gruppe das jiddische ‚Yidn‘ oder ‚erlicher Yidn‘. Die Identität wird aus Gottesfurcht und intensivem Torastudium gezogen. Der Mann, der Gott fürchtet, ist von ihm gesegnet. Dies bedeutet auch, dass die Halacha in ihrem Wortsinn und ohne Abstriche erfüllt und getan werden soll, womit ein Erwählungsbewusstsein einhergeht, nicht nur gegenüber „den Völkern", sondern auch gegenüber den assimilierten oder liberalen Juden. Ein dezidierter Skripturalismus wird vertreten, der in der Überzeugung kulminiert, dass das Tora -Studium dem Tempelopfer vorzuziehen ist. Die Haredim sprechen Jiddisch, auch wenn in den letzten Jahren das Neuhebräische zunehmend in ihre Kreise Einzug hielt. Ein konstantes Merkmal blieb die antizionistische Grundhaltung.

Behutsam entfaltet Herbasch im ersten Kapitel seiner Arbeit aus den Schlüsselmomenten der historischen Entwicklung Geschichte und Theologie des Chassidismus im Verhältnis zu der Chabad-Bewegung. Die Chassidim lehren eine elementarisierte Kabbala und richten sich damit an den durchschnittlichen Juden. Die Mitnagdim, die ostjüdische Urzelle der Haredim, hingegen behalten das kabbalistische Studium dem innersten Kreis der Eingeweihten vor, wobei sie die Kabbala nicht nur lehren, sondern auch zur Lebensform machen und in die Herzen einschreiben wollen. Diese kabbalistisch mystische Strömung des Judentums verbindet, wie erstmals Gershom Scholem in seinen großen Studien gezeigt hat, den jüdischen Monotheismus mit einer panentheistischen Dimension. Gott ist über allem und damit in allem, er ist das Heilige und das Profane. Offensichtlich entstehen von hier her Schwierigkeiten, diesen Panentheismus strikt von einem Pantheismus zu unterscheiden, der dem jüdischen Monotheismus widersprechen würde. In der, wie Herbasch es nennt, ‚theosophischen' Linie der Mitnagdim liegt auch die Haltung des ‚dvekut', die Vereinigung mit Gott, als erster Schritt der „unio mystica", welche in ‚bitul', der Selbstaufhebung des Menschen, enden soll.

Geschichte und Theologie der Chabad-Bewegung können vor dieser Folie klar dargestellt werden. Die unmittelbare rabbinische Genealogie setzt im 18. Jahrhundert mit Rabbi Schneur Zalman an und endet bis auf weiteres mit dem Tod des letzten Rebbe, Rabbi Schneerson im Alter von 92 Jahren im Jahr 1994. Schlüsselwerk ist das Buch ‚Tanya', das gleichermaßen für Lehre und Studium des Chassidismus und als Leitfaden der Spiritualität figuriert. Dieses Buch ist gleichermaßen Leitfaden zum Studium der Kabbalistik und Anleitung zur spirituellen Lebensform. Programmatisch ist bereits die Bezeichnung ‚Chabad', ein Akronym aus drei Worten: ‚hokhmah' (Weisheit); ‚binah' (Verstehen, Verstand) ‚daat' (Wissen). Benannt sind damit zugleich drei Stadien der Welt in Gott – von der Schöpfungsidee, über die Entfaltung bis hin zu ihrer Vollendung. Ein Grundgedanke von Chabad ist die göttliche Seele jedes Juden, ‚nefesh elochit', die neben der animalischen Seele (nehfesh bahamit) existiert. Die göttliche Seele ist gemäß kabbalistischer Lehre in der Lage, höhere Sphären (sefirot) zu sich herabzuziehen oder sich mit ihnen zu verbinden. Doch so wie die göttliche Seele in jedem Juden lebendig ist, so ist die animalische Seele auch in Gott.

In diesen kabbalistischen Rahmen fügt ‚Chabad' seine messianischen Erwartungen ein. Sie sind Teil der Hoffnung auf eine vollkommene, messianisch errettete Welt. Der messianische Zustand sei durch die Genealogie der Rebben vorbereitet worden. Manche Chabad-Anhänger sehen in Schneerson gar den Messias, der den Tod überwinden würde. Die von Scholem nahegelegte Unterscheidung zwischen einem utopisch katastrophischen und einem restaurativen Messianismus kann auf den Chabad-Messianismus nur bedingt abgebildet werden, weil er in die göttliche Eigenzeit eintritt und nicht geschichtlich utopisch orientiert ist. Er neigt freilich, wie Herbasch deutlich macht, eher zu der restaurativen Seite.

Das zweite Kapitel wendet sich nun den realpolitischen Berührungen von Chabad in Israel anhand von zwei Fallstudien zu. Höchst differenziert geht Herbasch auf die Debatte ein, die seit den fünfziger Jahren der Frage gilt, wer ein Jude sei. Mit ihr verbindet sich nämlich das Problem des Rückkehrrechts nach Israel. Die Darstellung gewinnt hier Spannung und

Plastizität, weil der Verfasser einzelne faktische Fälle von Einwanderern diskutiert und sie an den jeweiligen normativen Maßstäben misst. Ethnische, nationale und schließlich religiöse Diskursmuster überlagern sich gemäß dem ambivalenten Selbstverständnis im Judentum. Die Konversion zum Judentum gemäß der Anerkennung durch die orthodoxe Religionsbehörde hat sich dabei als Definitionsmacht herauskristallisiert. Schneerson, der Rebbe, liefert indessen, wie Herbasch zeigt, eine ganz eigenständige, rein spirituell mystische Begründung des Judeseins. Durch die Konversion und die Bindung an die Tora, nicht durch Abstammung und Nation, wird ein Mensch zum Juden. Seine unsterbliche Seele ist eine andere als die des Nicht-Juden. Der Konversion kommt dabei eine Art ‚character indelebilis' zu, der auch andauert für den Fall, dass die Person zu einer anderen Religionsgemeinschaft klonvertieren oder zum Agnostiker oder Atheisten werden sollte. Ein Jude ist also im Sinn von Chabad ein Mensch, in dessen Seele ein heiliger Funke wohnt, Teil des panentheistischen Gottes selbst. Für die Interkulturalität Israels und die Verbindung von säkularer und nicht-säkularer Weltsicht, die in politischen Diskussionen vorgebracht werden, ist es von großer Bedeutung, dass diese Position. ohne – wie es Habermas oder Rawls für liberale pluralistische Gesellschaften fordern – in eine säkular zugängliche Sprache übersetzt zu werden, in die politische Diskussion eingeht.

Ähnlich aufschlussreich ist das zweite gewählte Fallbeispiel: Der Sechs Tage-Krieg im Jahr 1967 mit seinen unerwarteten Gebietszuwächsen. Israel sah sich selbst wieder am Rand eines neuen Holocaust. Dass diese Katastrophe abgewendet werden konnte, führte ‚der Rebbe', Schneerson, auf Gottes Eingreifen zurück. Nicht aber auf die militärische Überlegenheit, sondern auf das Gebet und auf die Einwirkung Gottes selbst. Unter ‚nefesh pikuach', die Verpflichtung eines jeden Juden andere Menschen zu retten, kann die Gefährdung abgewiesen werden. In der Forschung ist, was Herbasch umsichtig referiert, bis heute umstritten, ob sich in diesem eigenwilligen Engagement von Chabad für Israel eine messianische Erwartung oder einfach höchste Gesetzestreue manifestiert. Die biblische Bedeutung des Heiligen Landes spielt für Chabad keine Rolle. Wohl aber wird auf die Verpflichtung jedes Juden hingewiesen, zur Sicherheit von Israel beizutragen. Israel ist dabei für Chabad ein säkularer Staat, wie jeder andere auch. Und Juden, die in Israel oder sogar in Jerusalem leben, leben nach wie vor im Exil (galut). Der Zustand der Erlösung (geulah) ist nur durch ein ALEPH, den Schöpfungsbuchstaben, von ‚galut' entfernt.

Das dritte Kapitel fragt, wie sich dies auf eines der umstrittensten Politikfelder in Israel, die Siedlungspolitik, auswirkt. Einem präzise recherchierten Überblick über die Siedlungspolitik schließt sich die höchst aufschlussreiche Vergleichsperspektive auf die Bewegung „Gush Emunim", eine Bewegung des religiösen Zionismus, an, die die Siedlungspolitik und Landnahme selbst messianisch begründet: Gott habe dieses Land für die Juden erwählt. Es wieder in Besitz zu nehmen, bedeutet daher, den Glauben an Gott auszuweiten. Toleranz gegenüber nicht-gläubigen Juden war nicht ausgeschlossen, und verband sich mit aggressiver Siedlungspolitik, wobei der Einfluss von Gush Emunim bis weit in das Zentrum der politischen Eliten Israels reicht und auch in den Biographien von Spitzenpolitikern wie Menachem Begin oder Ariel Sharon sichtbar wurde.

Die Toleranz erstreckt sich bekanntlich nicht auf die Araber, und auch nicht auf die nicht-jüdischen Völker, und ihr Einfluss reichte vor allem in den siebziger und frühen achtziger Jahren in die Macht-und Elitezentren der israelischen Politik.

Man hat damit ein exaktes Gegenbild der Chabad-Bewegung vor sich. Für sie nämlich ist das Heilige Land längst nicht mehr heilig. Nur durch die Heiligung der Juden, den göttlichen Funken, kann es gleichsam gereinigt werden. Auch hier ist noch einmal zu betonen, dass es für Chabad letztlich keine Rolle spielt, wo ein Jude lebt. Selbst im Heiligen Land kann man in der Knechtschaft sein, daraus ergibt sich eine paradoxe Struktur der Politischen Theologie von Chabad. Einerseits ist alles ‚galut' (Exil). Andererseits aber ist die Besiedelung Voraussetzung um das besetzte Land zu reinigen und dadurch die messianische Ankunft zu beschleunigen. In der politischen Positionierung resultiert daraus, dass Chabad keine aktive Siedlungspolitik betreibt, aber sehr aktiv die Siedlungspolitik unterstützt.

Herbasch berührt mit seiner äußerst validen Leitfrage nach den Gründen des Engagements ultraorthodoxer Juden in der Politik des säkularen Staates Israel ein in den letzten Jahren insbesondere von Michael Walzer thematisiertes Problemfeld: Walzer hat in seiner Studie ‚Exodus und Revolution' (1988) die jüdische Exodus-Politik seit der Wüstenwanderung herausgearbeitet. Die Wüstensituation und das „Murren des Volkes" sind dabei die maßgeblichen Motive, die zu einer allmählichen Verbesserung der Lebensverhältnisse im Zeichen des Exodus führen. Dies wird von Walzer ausdrücklich einer „messianischen" Politik entgegengesetzt, die immer eine Radikalisierung mit sich bringe und in säkularisierter Gestalt die totalitäre Politik des 20. Jahrhunderts immer wieder bestimmt habe. Walzer betont von hier her, auch gegenüber einem abstrakten, kultur-indifferenten

Liberalismus, dass Politik und Religion niemals klinisch rein voneinander zu scheiden sind. Wohl aber bedarf es einer subtilen Kunst der Unterscheidung, die es verhindert dass messianische Glut unmittelbar Politik bestimmend ist. Umso aufschlussreicher ist es vor diesem Hintergrund, einer seit dem Holocaust originär religiös messianischen Bewegung in ihrer politischen Aktivität zu begegnen.

Die Arbeit zeugt von hervorragender Sachkenntnis und von einer hervorragenden Verbindung von Sachlichkeit und Empathie. Die Komplexität und Vielstimmigkeit israelischer Debatten wird verständlicher. Dabei unternimmt Herbasch in keiner Weise eine Apologetik. Er versucht aber die immanente Logik von Chabad zu verstehen. Er zeigt die Sprengkraft und Eigendynamik und damit auch die Gefahr politischer Theologie, ohne zu werten, allein in dichten, plausiblen Beschreibungen. Doch er deutet auch an, wie sie in einen übergreifenden Diskurs eingebracht werden kann. Ihre Rationalität ist von anderer Art als die des liberalistischen Universalismus, der in der westlichen Welt dominiert. Doch jener Universalismus würde selbst ausschließend und reduktiv werden, wenn er die Dynamik religiöser Legitimatorik ausblenden wollte. In einem Land wie Israel dürfte sich diese Fiktion kaum halten lassen. Es gilt also den anderen zu verstehen: Dies leistet dieses schmale Buch in exemplarischer Weise. Es ist daher auch ein Beitrag zu dem Religionsfrieden, der für den Weltfrieden unerlässlich ist.

Basel, im Dezember 2013
Harald Seubert

Introduction

After centuries of Hasidism and the existence of the Habad movement, especially since the Seventh Rebbe took over the office as a leader of a disputable movement, there is still a lack of understanding for their political interest in Israel. *The Rebbe* is dead since 1994, but the Habad movement did in some sense not really notice a void. The movement is present in the Israeli politics as it was before the death of its charismatic leader. The modern State of Israel has been in existence for more than sixty years, she fought many wars, but survived it. The Habad movement sees in the State of Israel, more expressly in a state for Jews, more than one would as a non-Orthodox Jew.

What is the reason for Habad's interest in Israel? I base this paper on the interest of the Habad movement for Israel and its involvement in Israeli politics. What are the Habad movement's reasons to be concerned about the State of Israel?

Since the state came into existence, there are also scientific interests in politics and in religious meaning of the state, but to me there seems that to be a lack of discussion concerning the arguments which are used by the Habad movement to be involved, to even participate in matters of the state. One has to know that the Habad movement's headquarters are located in New York and that Habad is active world-wide. Why is it so concerned about the State of Israel? Even if, that has to be kept in mind from the beginning on, the Habad movement often declared that the actual existence of the State of Israel is not the beginning of redemption (in messianic terms) and it is not a Jewish state, but rather a state for Jews (in political terms).

Nonetheless, the Habad movement does care about the state for Jews. As a matter of fact, it is the place where the Holy Land once was/is, where many Jews reside and have to be saved from danger.

The Habad movement will be my subject for analysis as it proofs to be the most open(-minded) ultra-Orthodox group, sources for which are able for me to access. The theology of the Habad movement is very complex and paradox, though there is space for interpretation, the theology proofs to be concerned about the life of Jews and about the future of the world. The Messianism of the Habad movement is very clear in the sense that soon redemption will come with the coming of the Messiah. All these various reasons together play a very interesting and complex role, which is, finally, a clear answer – one in messianic matters and one in political reality.

I had wanted to know the answer for this question for a long time, therefore I am writing this paper to find the answer for myself and propose it to humanities for discussion, and to help enlarge knowledge about the movement and its reason for involvement.

In this paper I will cover the domestic issues and the international issues, each with one argument respectively. The last argument is supposed to be in-between international and domestic issues. The topics I choose are by no means taken arbitrarily. I rather took them with the intention to propose an answer for the respective issues, in how far the movement is involved and which religious arguments are taken into consideration by the movement.

However, before I concentrate on the actual involvement, it is necessary to define the ultra-Orthodox Jew and all the aspects which are important for the understanding of the forthcoming arguments, thereby the reader will understand how I see the discussion. After this I give a short overview about the history of Mitnaggdim, the opponents of Hasidim. The Habad movement was born out of Hasidism and one can still see the Habad movement as a part of the Hasidic denomination, therefore I examine not only the history of Hasidism, but also its theosophy. At the end I analyze the Habad movement; I will give a historical overview and an introduction to the Habadic theology.

Finally, afore I discuss my arguments in the second chapter, I have to clarify Messianism in an excursus as it is of importance for the understanding of the Habad movement.

The second chapter will begin with the discussion of the 'Who is a Jew?' debate, which still remains a very lively, colorful, and rich argument.

This argument already started in the early years of the existence of the State of Israel, as it was introduced with the introduction of the *Law of Return* in 1950. The *Law of Return* and the State of Israel had to face sundry claims to the application of the law. They differed on the question of its validity for former Jews, on the question of who may be registered under the *Population Registry Law*, and went on to questions of converts or Jews at the fringe of being Jews and not being taken as another religion.

The Habad movement, which I continue to discuss in this argument, faced the question from the beginning on that only the Halakhah has to decide about the issue and that if the Habad movement is asked it would only be valid for orthodox Jews or if it has to be applied for converts, in which case it would be but a halakhic, and thus correct conversion. This conversion has to happen under the supervision of an Orthodox Rabbi approved for conversions. I take as an example the informing pamphlet of Rabbi Jacob Immanuel Schochet and Habadnik, he poses at the end of his paper the unity of all Jews, which is not applicable for converts under non-Orthodox circumstances; but is of highest religious importance, which leads to the End of Times, the coming of the Messiah.

The next part of the second chapter is not so much based on domestic issues, but much more on international issues, and also covers the important topic war – the Six Day War. I shortly introduce the argument with the course of the war. Mostly, I analyze the foreseeing of the war by *the Rebbe* and his reaction to it by the appeal to pray with phylacteries (*tefillin*) which are steeped in religious significance. After the war the Habad movement was very concerned about the security of the State of Israel for the sake of the Jewish soul (*nefesh pikuach*), therefore the occupied territories have to be kept. Interestingly, *the Rebbe* excluded from his argumentation the Messianic meaning of the territories, though that is not to be taken seriously, as we will see. Thus I examine the relevance of the Six Day War and the territorial gains for Messianic purposes.

The third chapter is not only in-between domestic and international issues, as it deals not only with the settlement policy of the State of Israel in the occupied territories, but also compares the Habad movement with Gush Emunim (the bloc of faithful). Having discussed the development of the settlement policy in the territories after the Six Day War, I will analyze the history of Gush Emunim. Then I proceed with the *Weltanschauung* of the bloc by introducing its spiritual inspiration through the Rabbis Kook, and finally I examine the bloc's sometimes harsh settlement policy.

The Habad movement has a passive approach to settlements. At first I explain the factual unimportance of the State of Israel and the occupied territories in its mystical and seemingly Messianic appearance, as the whole world seems them to be the diaspora (*galut*); nonetheless the purification of the Holy Land is never wrong.

Further, I analyze Habad's approach based on facts of reality. *Nefesh pikuach* appears again. For this analysis I use, in spite of its polemical nature, the pamphlet of Eliyahu Touger recommended by the movement. He discusses the religious relevance of the occupied territories, however, in his whole paper the passive appeal for settlement can be felt. The result of the discussion about the Habad movement regarding settlement policy will be that it is a paradoxical approach in as far as its ambiguous messianic and reality-based argumentation is concerned.

For this paper I will be guided by various experts for the several fields. The actual researchers in the diverse realms will be mentioned according to my best knowledge.

For the religious part, we meet Immanuel Etkes, the expert in the early history of Hasidism and the genesis of Eastern European Orthodoxy, for instance the *Gaon of Vilna*. Of course, there are many more, which should be added, but due to a lack of space I have to go over to the next field.

For the twentieth century I will cite as experts Aviezer Ravitzky, Samuel Heilman, Menachem Friedman, Mark Avrum Ehrlich, and Eliezer Don-Yehiya; but also Benjamin Brown, who mainly wrote in Hebrew. All of them based their research mainly on history and political science; nonetheless they all have a huge knowledge in religious and philosophical realms. Knowing that it is only possible to mention a part of the experts, I think I named at least the most famous scholars.

Philosophy is, however, more the field of Rachel Elior who describes in perfect and well taken words the theosophic and philosophic ideologies of ultra-Orthodoxy in Judaism. One must not forget Elliot R. Wolfson, another one who has a profound knowledge about theosophy, Jewish philosophy and Kabbalah in relation to Judaism. This is also the case for Moshe Idel and Joseph Dan, two experts in the field of the (Jewish) Kabbalah. Naftali Loewenthal has also a very interesting view on the early philosophic and theosophic discussion in the Habad movement.

In the end it is always a list which could be extended with experts in every field, one would only have to change the names in the above-mentioned categories.

Due to a lack of sources I dare to present my own interpretation in the second part of the third chapter. Furthermore I am forced to take articles of journalists into consideration in the coverage of the settlement policy; this is all based on lack of more up-to-date sources.

Chapter I: Definition of Ultra-Orthodoxy

1. Haredim

In almost every paper about Orthodox Jews, ultra-Orthodox Jews, or *Haredim*, it does not matter which kind of paper, there is a new definition of the term *ultra-Orthodox Jew*. There is not any kind of agreement between scholars to agree once and for all on a final definition of the term.

Established scholars, like, inter alia, Benjamin Brown, Eliezer Don-Yehiya, Aviezer Ravitzky, Samuel C. Heilman, Menachem Friedman, or the historian of Hungarian Jewry Michael K. Silber,[1] do not agree in most of their vocabulary on the definition of *ultra-Orthodoxism* or *Haredism*. It does not matter how the contradictions are expressed, the fact that they are continually disputed in numerous works is reason enough to define these terms anew. Nevertheless, I will model my definition mainly on the one created by Heilman.[2]

First of all, why do I use the Hebrew term Haredim instead of the well-known term ultra-Orthodox? The sources for this neologism is the Torah. Haredi (or Haredim in plural) means, firstly, *one who trembles*, according to

---

[1] See, inter alia, Eliezer Don-Yehiya, "Traditionalist Strands," in *Modern Judaism: an Oxford Guide*, ed. Nicholas Robert Michael De. Lange and Miri Freud-Kandel (Oxford, New York: Oxford University Press, 2005), 93-105. As well Samuel C. Heilman and Menachem Friedman, "Religious Fundamentalism and Religious Jews - The Case of Haredim," in *Fundamentalisms Observed*, ed. Martin E. Marty and R. Scott Appleby, *The Fundamentalism Project* (Chicago: The University of Chicago Press, 1991), 197-264. Further definitions are found in Nurit Stadler, *Yeshiva fundamentalism* (New York, London: New York University Press, 2009). 1-51. Additionally in Aviezer Ravitzky, *Messianism, Zionism, and Jewish religious radicalism* (Chicago [u.a.]: Univ. of Chicago Press, 1996). 145-80. In my view is the definition of Silber very explaining, see Michael K. Silber, "The Emergence of Ultra-Orthodoxy - The Invention of a Tradition," in *The uses of tradition - Jewish continuity in the modern era*, ed. Jack Wertheimer (New York: Jewish Theol. Seminary of America u.a., 1992), 26. A very good definiton is given by Benjamin Brown, "Orthodox Judaism," in *The Blackwell Companion to Judaism*, ed. Jacob Neusner and Alan J. Avery-Peck, *Blackwell Companions to Religion* (Oxford: Blackwell Publishers Ltd, 2000). There are of course many more definitions, though it is enough for the beginning to show the *variétés* of definitions of the ultra-Orthodox adherents.

[2] See Samuel C. Heilman, *Defenders of the Faith - Inside Ultra-Orthodox Jewry* (Berkley, Los Angeles, London: University of California Press, 1992).

Isaiah 66:5 "Hear the word of the Lord, ye that tremble at his word."[3] It is located in Ezra 10:3, too: "And of those that tremble at the commandment of our God."[4]

Secondly, as David Landau highlights, and he is by far not the only one, by referring to a different meaning of Haredim: *for those who fear H-m*.[5] It is absolutely important to put the *fear of G-d* into the foreground. Not only small male children of Haredim (*tinokos shel bais rabban*, the children of the rabbis' school)[6] have to internalize the Psalm 111:10 "The fear of the Lord is the beginning of wisdom."[7] *G-dfear* is an essential meaning of Haredim. Thus, Haredim are people who tremble and fear G-d, including *yiras shomayim*, the fear of Heaven.

The approach of the Habad movement is a proper example that serves as an explanation for *Haredism*. The sixth Lubavitcher Rebbe, the Rebbe Yosef Yitzchak Schneerson (the *frierdiker Rebbe*/the former Rebbe) set as the first step for Divine service the *yiras shomayim*, the fear of Heaven. The fear was connected with a phrase of the *Zohar*[8] which declared: "This (fear of G-d) is the gateway to all spiritual heights." – therefore the 'gateway to Heaven.' The *frierdiker Rebbe* went on and derived from that, that if there was no fear, there would be no wisdom, as the *Sages*[9] comment: "Anyone whose fear of sin comes before his wisdom, his wisdom will endure."[10]

The ultra-Orthodox Jews did not oft use Haredim or ultra-Orthodox Jew as a self-description; they preferred to describe themselves in Yiddish as *Yidn* or *erlicher Yidn* (virtuous Jews) in the meaning, someone who "observe[s] the Torah and its commandments".[11] The *erlicher Yidn*[12] saw them-

---

[3] Robert Carroll and Stephen Pricket, eds., *The Bible - Authorized King James Version with Apocrypha* (Oxford, New York: Oxford University Press, 1997).

[4] Ibid.

[5] See David Landau, *Piety and Power - The World of Jewish Fundamentalism* (New York: Hill and Wang, 1993).

[6] Citation taken from Heilman, *Defenders of the Faith - Inside Ultra-Orthodox Jewry*: 157.

[7] Carroll and Pricket, *The Bible - Authorized King James Version with Apocrypha*.

[8] The *Zohar* is the most important work of the Kabbalah. It was written in the Middle Ages and serves until today as a source for various denominations in Judaism.

[9] Any references to the Sages/Sanhedrin are usually meant to refer to the *Sanhedrin* of the time of the Second Temple.

[10] Cf Rebbe Yosef Yitzchak Schneerson, "Chassidic Discourses - Chapter IV," Kehot Publication Society, http://www.chabad.org/library/article_cdo/aid/73656/jewish/Chapter-IV.htm. [06/14/2012].

[11] Heilman and Friedman, "Religious Fundamentalism and Religious Jews - The Case of Haredim," 199.

selves not as a sect or an obscure movement, but in absolute contrast to those Jews who were emancipated or enlightened: they, the ultra-Orthodox Jews, are the true ones with the so-called pious *Yidishkeit* (Jewishness). "If they are indeed haredim, then it must mean that to them there is something essentially Jewish about being haredi and something essentially haredi about being Jewish. To the haredim, this truth is beyond question."[13]

Above I presented the terminological usage of Haredim. Now I cover the historical development of Haredim, in detail I present the relevant denominations for this paper. At first, I give a common overview.

Initially, one has to pay special attention to Eastern Europe in the eighteenth and nineteenth century, but one also has to focus on events in central Europe to understand the history of Jewry in Eastern Europe. It is, albeit, absolutely clear that Jewry was only confronted in central Europe with the beginning of modernity and secularity. These circumstances, that took place in central Europe, never became reality in the same harshness in Eastern Europe.[14]

But one has to wonder when examining this era about the disagreement in academic research concerning the origins of ultra-Orthodoxy as a movement within Jewry. We find the most disagreements or conscious (?) neglects about several groups in the Haredi sector.

They may be as obvious as the Hasidic part in Eastern Europe or as difficult to locate as the *Musar* (ethics) movement of Rabbi Israel Salanter in Lithuania.[15] Though there are various places in which ultra-Orthodoxy showed its face for different reasons. As there is in Eastern Europe: especially today's Lithuania with Vilna (today: Vilnius) in its center at the end of the eighteenth century, and further we locate Ukraine as the birthplace of Hasidism, also a creation of the eighteenth century.

Then we proceed with in Hungary; in this country the ultra-Orthodox Jews defined themselves through refusal to assimilate in Hungarian culture. This happened in the nineteenth century. At last, in Germany, also in

---

[12] According to Benjamin Brown, Haredim did use as a self-description as well Haredim, *Yereim* (God-fearers), and *Shlomei Emunei Israel* (Israelites of Wholehearted Faith). Cf Brown, "Orthodox Judaism," 312.

[13] Heilman and Friedman, "Religious Fundamentalism and Religious Jews - The Case of Haredim," 199.

[14] Cf Don-Yehiya, "Traditionalist Strands," 95.

[15] For further information about the Mussar Movement see the fantastic book of Immanuel Etkes, *Rabbi Israel Salanter and the Mussar Movement - Seeking the Torah of Truth*, trans. Jonathan Chipman (Philadelphia: Jewish Publication Society, 1993).

the nineteenth century, we meet Rabbi Samson Raphael Hirsch and R. Esriel Hildesheimer with their neo-Orthodoxy. The last two named strands are related to the *Haskalah* (Jewish Enlightenment) by opposing its views. In other words, they are descended disciples of rabbis who opposed the Jewish Enlightenment movement.

Secondly, out of historic circumstances there was a renaissance of *ultra-Orthodoxism* in the post-Shoa era. This was a rebirth not only because of the *Endlösungsplan* of *Nazi-Deutschland*. "Before the Second World War, many of the centers of Judaism in Eastern Europe had been disrupted by the Communist Revolution [in 1917]."[16] In the years from 1921 to 1924 the Jews suffered most under the newly erected Soviet Government, because it "began [with a] systematic eradication of Jewish religious observance."[17] Notwithstanding the fact that "nearly all of Russia's Jewish leaders had fled,"[18] many Jews remained in their homes because of concerns of their rabbis or several other reasons, to be enumerated as follows: They did not flee or migrate to the United States of America or today's Israel. "The most Orthodox had until the very end for the most part refused to go either to America, which they considered a place that swallowed up Jewish life (the *trefe medina* [an *unkosher* state], they called it), or Palestine, which they often saw as a holy land being desecrated by socialists and infidels."[19] I want to highlight the worries of the *Frierdiker Rebbe*, Rabbi Yosef Yitzhak Schneerson. He "maintained an anti-emigration policy. He insisted that there were enough Habad followers around the world to build the movement there, and that Judaism in Russia was in much greater need of qualified leadership than communities elsewhere, especially in the United States. He further insisted that those of his followers who left Russia were tantamount to deserters."[20] Nevertheless, there were a few members who ignored these objections and fled, as we shall see later. Due to the appearance of these circumstances and the destruction caused by the Second World War, almost all Jews in Eastern Europe were extinguished.

---

[16] Mark Avrum Ehrlich, *The Messiah of Brooklyn - Understanding Lubavitch Hasidism Past and Present* (Jersey City: KTAV Publishing House, 2004). 27.

[17] Ibid., 25.

[18] Ibid.

[19] Heilman and Friedman, "Religious Fundamentalism and Religious Jews - The Case of Haredim," 219-20.

[20] Ehrlich, *The Messiah of Brooklyn - Understanding Lubavitch Hasidism Past and Present*: 26.

The *renaissance* took place especially in the United States and in the newly founded State of Israel. The persons who survived the war and the cruelties of the Soviet Regime finally went to these states to build up new communities. Today there are politically powerful ultra-Orthodox communities in Israel.[21] In the States, there are big Jewish communities in New York City; in this city the largest diaspora-Jewish population in the world resides.[22] I only mention the 'headquarters' of the Habad movement in Brooklyn, in Crown Heights, 770 Eastern Parkway, known as Seven-Seventy. According to Mark Avrum Ehrlich about 20,000 Habad members lived in this area in 1988.[23]

I continue describing the typical characteristics of Haredim; I refer mostly to currently existing ultra-Orthodox groups. Foremost, I start with the religious observance; as one may expect the Haredim are very strict and stringent in their observance of the 613 commandments (*Taryag mitzvoth* (commandments), as it is called in Hebrew). *Taryag* represents the numbers of commandments which are written in the Torah. As a logical consequence ultra-Orthodox Jews orient their lives toward G-d. However, Haredim see themselves as chosen by H-m and therefore it is consistent for them to implement the Halakah[24] as perfectly as possible. This process is achieved mainly through prayer and Torah study. The modern world is also taken into consideration, because, alongside the development of Haredim, ultra-Orthodox Jews need the modern world to feel 'more' to be the Chosen Ones – in contrast to secular Jews or gentiles. It is an elitist self-

---

[21] Their political power can be seen in all governments in Israel, because the ultra-Orthodox parties almost always tip the scales.

[22] Cf Ehrlich, *The Messiah of Brooklyn - Understanding Lubavitch Hasidism Past and Present*: 144. According to the North American Jewish Databank, a survey published stating that the Jewish population of the State of New York represents 8.4 % of the total population. Further, the Jewish population numbers 1,635,000.
Cf Ira M. Sheshkin and Arnold Dashefsky, "Jewish Population in the United States 2011," North American Jewish Data Bank, http://www.jewishdatabank.org/Reports/-Jewish_Population_in_the_United_States_2011.pdf. [06/14/2012].

[23] Cf Ehrlich, *The Messiah of Brooklyn - Understanding Lubavitch Hasidism Past and Present*: 139. About the present Habad population is no survey published. Though Lisa Beyer of the Time Magazine wrote in 1992 an article about the Habad movement and mentioned 30,000 followers residing in Brooklyn.
Cf Lisa Beyer, "Expecting the Messiah," The Rick Ross Institute Internet Archives, http://www.rickross.com/reference/lubavitch/lubavitch18.html. [06/19/2012].

[24] Halakah contains the observance of the 613 commandments and Talmudic and rabbinical laws.

image, as Friedman calls it. Finally, I cite R. Schlesinger one of the first Hungarian ultra-Orthodox Jews, according to him, they, the Haredim, are in the world to praise G-d. Therefore a Jew has to be incompetent in worldly matters, as for example in matters of natural science. The roles and consequently the vocational goals of Jews and non-Jews (*goyim*) are separate. On the one hand the nations (*goyim*) have been placed by G-d on earth to master it; they may do this by inventing new technologies, understanding nature and promoting the sciences. On the other hand, the Jews are the Chosen People and therefore have been placed by G-d on earth to study Torah, to do mitzvoth, and to pray for the world's well-being. All of these procedures are duly marked in the stringent guide of R. Schlesinger.[25] There are additional inventions of traditions.

The ultra-Orthodox Jew has to think of himself to be a Haredi, like the meaning demands. "Blessed is the man that feareth the Lord, that delighteth greatly in his commandments. His seed shall be mighty upon earth: the generation of the upright shall be blessed."[26] In other words, a Haredi is "the man who truly and completely fears God and greatly desires his 'mitzvot' *does not look for ways to free himself from the mitzvot nor does he seek out* 'qulot' [leniencies, the opposite of *humrot* (stringent interpretations)] and 'heteirim' [relaxations of restrictions], *but rather fulfills the halakhah as it is, without consideration*, and because of this he is assured that his seed will be mighty upon earth. [Emphasis in original]"[27] We see a true Haredi seeks to fulfill his life by accomplishing *mitzvoth*. Thus one of the characteristics of a Haredi is the orientation on the written laws which prescribe his way of life *a priori*. Any deviances only happen, if the modern world demands it, and new traditions have to be invented; as it happened recently in Israel in December 2011 and January 2012 concerning the separation of women and men in busses and in shops, to mention only these two. Its peak was reached when a demonstration of ultra-Orthodox Jews donned Star of David patches mostly combined with prison garbs to evoke

---

[25] Cf Silber, "The Emergence of Ultra-Orthodoxy - The Invention of a Tradition," 63.

[26] Carroll and Pricket, *The Bible - Authorized King James Version with Apocrypha*, Ps. 112,1-2.

[27] Rabbi Israel Meir Ha-Cohen (the Hafetz Haim), citation taken from Menachem Friedman, "Life Tradition and Book Tradition in the Development of Ultraorthodox Judaism," in *Judaism viewed from within and from without*, ed. Harvey E. Goldberg (Albany: State University of New York Press, 1987), 239.

the memory of the Second World War and the cruelties done by the Nazis to Jews.[28]

At least on the point of traditionalism all scholars agree on definitions about ultra-Orthodoxy; that out of stringent religious observance results a deep sense of affection for tradition. Haredim are not bare traditionalists, as they are often called, they invented traditions. To be sure, they used a more stringent *halakhic* (Jewish law) concept than was demanded.[29] The tradition alone even in its most strict fulfillment of the *Halakhah* is not enough today for a Haredi to be an ultra-Orthodox Jew; he must be able to consider the different facets of modern life and include it in his practice. Albeit, there has been a rupture with the Shoa and antisemitic pre-Shoa attacks which delegitimized tradition and led in the post-Holocaust period to *Scripturalism*, to be explained next. But notwithstanding all these horrible events, the secularization of modern Europe played its role in creating a break in Jewish culture[30] and made it more than legitimate to pray more

---

[28] See inter alia Isabel Kershner, "Israeli Girl, 8, at Center of Tension Over Religious Extremism," The New York Times, http://www.nytimes.com/2011/12/28/-world/middleeast/israeli-girl-at-center-of-tension-over-religious-extremism.html?_r=1&sq=ultra%20orthodox%20israel&st=cse&scp=2&pagewanted=all. [01/09/2012]. Robert Mackey to The Lede, 2011, http://thelede.blogs.nyti-mes.com/2011/12/28/the-israeli-tv-report-on-gender-segregation-that-sparked-pro-test/?scp=3&sq=ultra%20orthodox%20israel&st=cse. [01/09/2012]. unknown, dpa, and AFP, "Ultraorthodoxe randalieren in Beit Schemesch," Zeit Online, http://w-ww.zeit.de/politik/ausland/2011-12/israel-ultra-orthodoxe. [01/09/2012]. unk-nown, dpa, and AFP, "Ultraorthodoxe Juden vergleichen Israel mit Nazi-Reich," Zeit Online, http://www.zeit.de/politik/ausland/2012-01/ultraorthodoxe-israel-prot-est. [01/09/2012]. Yair Ettinger, "Hundreds of ultra-Orthodox Jews protest in Jerusalem against 'exclusion of Haredim'," Haaretz.com, http://www.haaretz.com/-news/national/hundreds-of-ultra-orthodox-jews-protest-in-jerusalem-against-exc-lusion-of-haredim-1.404783. [01/09/2012]. Oz Rosenberg, "Hundreds of ultra-Orthodox protesters riot in flashpoint town of Beit Shemesh," Haaretz.com, http://www.haaretz.com/news/national/hundreds-of-ultra-orthodox-protesters-riot-in-flashpoint-town-of-beit-shemesh-1.404470. [01/09/2012]. Anshel Pfeffer, "Jerusalem's public transport system as metaphor for Israel in 2012," Haaretz.com, http://www.haaretz.com/print-edition/news/jerusalem-s-public-transport-system-as-metaphor-for-israel-in-2012-1.405732. [01/09/2012].

[29] Cf Friedman, "Life Tradition and Book Tradition in the Development of Ultraorthodox Judaism," 236.

[30] Cf Benjamin Beit-Hallahmi and Zvi Sobel, "Introduction," in *Traditon, Innovation, Conflict - Jewishness and Judaism in Contemporary Israel*, ed. Benjamin Beit-Hallahmi and Zvi Sobel (Albany: State University of New York, 1991), 5.

intensely because of the lost flock (the secular Jews). In other words, ultra-Orthodox Jews created their own laws and sealed it as tradition. In fact, it is a new law, but they claim it is from then on an ever-lasting tradition, which can be traced back to Moses, when they have to legitimize it. A very noteworthy example is the *Hatam Sofer*[31] (b. 1762 – d. 1839) who held the last generation in greater esteem than the next generation. In a discussion the rabbi issued a statement that exemplifies the Haredi culture very succinctly. He unified the earlier and later generations into one organic body ("For the son is a part of his father and rooted in him."[32]), and by doing this he justified his halakhic conclusion that "the sons' authority to annul a vow was less than that of their fathers in establishing it."[33] One sees, indeed, how the past was worth more than the present. It works still today. Nathaniel Deutsch cites one member of the Satmar Hasidic community in Williamsburg, Brooklyn: "No one is interested in modern culture. We have a saying … 'Don't be smarter than your father'"[34]

Haredi Jews base their lives on a culture of yesteryear, which has more authority than the possibilities of today, thus it is easier to accept the lived life. Haredim "consider their lives as a service to God and Jewish tradition and the only true merit that which is prescribed by the Torah and its accepted rabbinic interpretations."[35]

"The Study of Torah is greater than the daily sacrifices of the Temple,"[36] – this saying introduces not only the second chapter of Nurit Stadler's book 'Yeshiva Fundamentalism,'[37] but also properly introduces *Scripturalism*. The saying highlights the importance of the strict and stringent implementation of consequent and lasting Torah study. Nevertheless, a very strict following of this *mitzvah* is an invention of the post-Shoa communities in the coun-

---

[31] The *Hatam Sofer* got famous for his cunning phrase: "*Col Haddash Asur min ha-Torah*" (Everything new is forbidden by the Torah).

[32] Cited in Jakob Katz, "Towards a Biography of the Hatam Sofer," in *From East and West - Jews in a Changing Europe, 1750 - 1870*, ed. Francis Malino and David Sorkin (London: Blackwell Publishing, 1990), 253.

[33] Ibid.

[34] Nathaniel Deutsch, "The Forbidden Fork, the Cell Phone Holocaust, and Other Haredi Encounters with Technology," *Contemporary Jewry* 29, no. 1 (2009): 4.

[35] Samuel C. Heilman and Fred Skolnik, "Haredim," in *Encyclopaedia Judaica*, ed. Michael Berenbaum and Fred Skolnik (Detroit: Macmilan, 2007), 349.

[36] Babylonian Talmud, Megilah 3b. Citation taken from Stadler, *Yeshiva fundamentalism*: 35.

[37] A *Yeshiva* is a Jewish Talmud school.

tries with former East-European ultra-Orthodox Jews. In other words these former Eastern-Europeans developed an extreme and stringent following of the *Halakhah*, but it is possible mainly in Israel to find Scripturalism. According to Stadler, Scripturalism regards the holy books as written basis for fundamentalist[38] groups.[39] Though, in general it is important for any Haredi adherent to take the study of holy books as essential: "For example [has been given] the commandment in Deuteronomy 6:7 to study Torah 'when you sit at home and when you walk abroad' ... absolute centrality."[40]

In other words, Haredim see themselves as responsible to re-erect the destroyed (ultra-Orthodox) Jewry caused by the Shoa and the cruelties in the Soviet areas, as in these times the Jewish belief was delegitimized by outer forces. Mordecai Bar-Lev highlights this in his article about *Jewish Religious Education* in Israel. He mentions the Holocaust as a major dilemma for the *Yeshivot*, but draws attention to the survivors of the Shoa who "sought to perpetuate the memory of their loved ones by 'setting a yeshiva on their graves,' similar to the traditional yeshiva destroyed in the Holocaust."[41]

The *Scripturalism* is primarily achieved through the extensive construction of new *Yeshivot* and lengthened studying of the *Seforim* (holy books) by the male section of the Haredi community. The strict observance of studying the Torah for the sake of the Jews murdered in the Shoa compensates the sins of the *Hilonim* (secular Jews) and led to many problems in Israel.

The Marker, the economic newspaper of *Haaretz*, alerts that Israel may still be able to defend itself in 20 years, without many Haredim and Israelis

---

[38] I orientate the definition of fundamentalism on the definition of Karsten Fischer. He demands that fundamentalism is a kind of protest movement in relation to religious politics, based on the anger against modernity-processes. Fundamentalists who are the product of fundamentalism agree with the base of revelation as authority in an apocalyptic approach. In conclusion, fundamentalism is a relational phenomenon to secular modernity in an elitist way. Cf Karsten Fischer, "Fundamentalismus," in *Politische Theorie und Politische Philosophie - Ein Handbuch*, ed. Martin Hartmann and Claus Offe (München: C.H. Beck, 2011), 193.

[39] Cf Stadler, *Yeshiva fundamentalism*: 8.

[40] Ibid., 9.

[41] Mordecai Bar-Lev, "Tradition and Innovation in Jewish Religious Education in Israel," in *Tradition, Innovation, Conflict - Jewishness and Judaism in Contemporary Israel*, ed. Benjamin Beit-Hallahmi and Zvi Sobel (Albany: State University of New York, 1991), 117.

of Palestinian origin.[42] Though, Israel will get problems in the macroeconomic field.[43] Haredim were exempted from the draft to IDF (Israel Defense Forces) because of the so-called *Tal law*, which is mainly based on the 'Status Quo' agreement. This agreement was passed in 1953.[44] It is obvious that Scripturalism will lead to major hassles in Israel's future, if this practice of all Haredi men dedicating themselves exclusively to study the Torah continues.

Further, Haredim show insularity by speaking Yiddish as their vernacular; they use it primarily at least within their own communities. Nevertheless, Hebrew takes more and more turf in the world of Haredim, because outside of their community most people speak Hebrew. The Haredi youth has gotten used to speaking Hebrew. Insularity per se is unmistakably beheld in the living of Haredim in their clear-cut neighborhoods.[45] This insularity is definitely a landmark of the ultra-Orthodox communities. There are many more facts to be enumerated which symbolize this insularity. As there were two school systems established through the 'Status Quo' Agreement, a general one and a religious one for Haredi children. Of course I do not forget alluding to their outer appearance on the streets all around the world, not only in Israel, with their black caftans, long and unkempt beards, and *payot* (sidelocks). The black coat is seen as a sign of mourning for the destruction of the Second Temple in 70 CE by the Romans.[46] Haredi women have a similar appearance, albeit with more color, though with kerchiefs, hats or wigs on their sometimes shaven heads, to mention only a few of their outward markings.

---

[42] I do not further discuss the topic about the Arab/Palestinian situation in Israel.

[43] Cf Elad Dor and Nati Tucker, "Arabs, Haredim not working will become macro danger," The Marker.com, http://english.themarker.com/arabs-haredim-not-working-will-become-macro-danger-1.323886. [01/09/2012].

[44] Cf Eran Kaplan, "Israeli Jewry," in *Modern Judaism: An Oxford Guide*, ed. N.R.M.D. Lange and Miri Freud-Kandel (Oxford, New York: Oxford University Press, 2005), 144-46.

[45] Cf Don-Yehiya, "Traditionalist Strands," 94.

[46] Every strand of the Haredim communities wears a different kind of caftan. Outsiders of the Haredi world are usually not able to discern differences in the garments. Simeon D. Baumel agrees: "To the untrained eye, the haredi world often looks like a monolith of black hats and white shirts. Insiders, however, can distinguish between the various groups in the blink of an eye, through different dress codes, behavioral patterns, and, of course, cultural and philosophical differences." Simeon D. Baumel, "Weekly Torah Portions, Languages, and Culture among Israeli Haredim," *Jewish Social Studies* 10, no. 2 (2004): 155.

This Insularitism, in summary, is highlighted by the Haredim decision to *ghettoize* their communities and their lives. As seen above, it happens through avoidance of modernity, their garments, their tongue Yiddish, and their special treatment in the Israeli society.

The last characteristic of Haredim is a fact wherein all ultra-Orthodox communities of every *couleur* agree: anger against Zionism.

It has to be clear from the start that most of Haredim opposed Zionism, because they saw in it a humanly based attempt to try to hasten redemption. Some factions in the Haredi communities opposed Zionism because of the dominance of secular Jews and their nationalistic and secular ideology which was taken as a replacement of the Torah and its Commandments; many saw it as *avodah zarah* (idolatry).[47] "The leading east European rabbis regarded it as unmitigated disaster, a poisonous weed, more dangerous even than Reform Judaism, hitherto regarded as the main menace."[48]

Nevertheless, Haredim also had to face reality and founded *Agudat Israel in 1912*,[49] but one can see in their first declaration that they are far away from being pleased at the behavior of Zionists – *Agudat Israel* was a clear Haredi declaration of pure anti-Zionism. However, the time demanded adaptations with the Balfour Declaration in 1917, the Shoa and the foundation of Eretz Israel in 1948, as there harsh arguments in *Agudat* were raised.

Isaac Breuer (b. 1833 – d. 1946) founded the more pro-Zionistic association *Poalei Agudat Israel* (the workers of *Agudat Israel*) in 1930.[50] Breuer gave a speech in 1934 in which he confronted *Agudat Israel* with the accusation of a neglect of Palestine. Breuer mentioned further, "if Aguda really wanted to combat Zionism it had again to become part of Jewish history, to prepare the Jewish homeland and the Jewish people for their reunion under the rule of the Torah. This was the will of divine providence which orthodox Jewry could afford to ignore only at the risk of its own existence."[51]

In effect, *Agudat Israel* got more and more pro-Eretz Israel (but not pro-Zionism). This was also a prelude for the 'Status Quo' agreement, as the

---

[47] Cf Don-Yehiya, "Traditionalist Strands," 97.

[48] Walter Laqueur, *A History of Zionism - From the French Revolution to the Establishment of the State of Israel* (New York: Schocken Books, 2003). 407.

[49] Agudat-Israel, "Zum Programm der Agudas Jisroel," in *The Jew in the Modern World - A Documentary History*, ed. Paul R. Mendes-Flohr and Jehuda Reinharz (New York, Oxford: Oxford University Press, 1980).

[50] Cf Don-Yehiya, "Traditionalist Strands," 99.

[51] Laqueur, *A History of Zionism - From the French Revolution to the Establishment of the State of Israel*: 411.

members of the Haredi association negotiated concessions with the Palestinian Zionist leaders about one year before the establishment of Israel; these were Shabbat observance, dietary laws, the school system, and marriage matters.[52]

In summation, the characteristics of Haredim are the strict observance of *taryag mitzvoth* with all its considerations, the self-assessment of the *erlicher Yidn* to be the real Chosen Ones, accompanied by Traditionalism (with the invention of new traditions), Scripturalism (but mainly performed in Israel), and Insularitism, which shows the outer appearances of ultra-Orthodox Jewry in its respective light. In the end anti-Zionism connects all Haredi *couleurs*. Zionism was not only jointly responsible for the naming as ultra-Orthodox Jews or Haredim, it was also seen by Haredim as a man-made redemption that must be clearly negated.

2. History of Mitnaggdim

On the next pages I cover the history of certain Haredi denominations which are relevant for the understanding of this paper. I begin with the Mitnaggdim (Opponents) which were let by the *Gaon of Vilna* (Genius of Vilna; R. Elijah ben Shlomon Zalman Kramer; b. 1720 – d. 1797) and will go with the *Besht* (*Baal Shem Tov* – Master of the Good Name; R. Yisreal ben Eliezer; b. 1698 – d. 1760), the founding father of Hasidism.

Mitnaggdim[53] (literally opponents) solely came into existence, as an opposition to Hasidim. The most influential of them was the *Gaon of Vilna* (b. 1720 – d. 1797), who was esteemed also by his enemies and his student Hayyim of Volozhin.

The *Gaon* was very concerned about the appearance of Hasidim in his environment. Immanuel Etkes, who wrote an excellent book about the *Gaon of Vilna*, grappled with this topic and came to a very convincing conclusion. The persons around the *Gaon* and especially the *Gaon* himself saw themselves as the true faithful traditionalists who had to fight for their worthwhile tradition.

The Hasidim, in contrast, deviated from the tradition, therefore they were, in the eyes of the *Gaon*, who was seen as the only one who was able

---

[52] Cf ibid., 413. See for the text of the 'Status-Quo' Agreement Itamar Rabinovich and Jehuda Reinharz, eds., *Israel in the Middle East - Documents and Readings on Society, Politics, and Foreign Relations, Pre-1948 to the Present*, Second ed. (London, Hanover: Brandeis University Press, 2008), 58-59.

[53] Today they are mostly called Lituanim after their origin in Lithuania.

to judge, heretics.[54] One has to know that the *Gaon* probably acted primarily out of "spiritual and religious motives rather than [out of] social and political reasons."[55] This means that the *Gaon* feared that Hasidism may lead to a renewal of Messianism, as it happened with Shabbatai Zvi,[56] because in 1772 it was just about twenty years after the Frankists had gone through Europe with their messianic ideas. What led the *Gaon* to such far reaching assumptions?

The approach of a Hasidic Jew may have been seen in the *Gaon's* mind as too far away from tradition. His tradition consisted of *Torah Lishmah*, the study of Torah for the sake of the Torah. The scholar Shimon Dubnow was convinced that "the aim of Hasidism was essentially to challenge the scholarly foundation of religion."[57] But the scholarly approach was highly valued in the tradition surrounding the *Gaon of Vilna*. The Hasidim, in contrast, replaced the traditional approach of *Torah Lishmah* with "emotion and devotion in the observance of commandments."[58] This was a deviation which could not be endured by the *Gaon*; he was absolutely angered[59] and

---

[54] Cf Immanuel Etkes, *The Gaon of Vilna - The Man and His Image*, trans. Jeffrey M. Green (Berkely, Los Angeles: University of California Press, 2002). 95.

[55] Ibid., 93.

[56] Cf Joseph Dan, *Die Kabbala - Eine kleine Einführung*, trans. Christian Wiese (Ditzingen: Reclam, 2007). 122-23.

[57] Etkes, *The Gaon of Vilna - The Man and His Image*: 74.

[58] Ibid.

[59] Etkes cited a source which is article six in the anthology *Zemir' Aritsim Ve-harvot Tsurim* (The Pruning Hook and Swords of Flint), published in 1772. The researcher thinks it is reliable because of its systematic and detailed survey of the events in Vilna. The worries of the *Gaon* are described as follows: "And when our rabbi and teacher Mendel of Minsk [a Hasid] was here last winter with the true Gaon, the man of God, our master and rabbi, Rabbi Eliyahu the Hasid, may his candle be bright, he did not see the face of the Gaon all that winter long. He [the *Gaon*] said that he had a commentary on a passage in the Zohar composed by their sect, in which there was heresy. … And when the writings arrived from Shklov here in the holy congregation of Vilna, the Gaon said: The holy congregation of Shklov is right, and as for the aforementioned sect, they are heretics and must be brought low." In a letter of R. Shneur Zalman of Lyady, a person we will meet more often in this paper, as he is the first Rebbe of the Habad community, and a former student of the *Besht*, referred to a similar situation at this time. "We went to the Gaon he-Hasid, may his candle burn brightly, to his house to debate with him and to remove his complaints from us, while I was there with the Hasid rabbi our late teacher Rabbi Mendel Horosener of blessed memory, and the Gaon closed his door before us twice. And when the great people of the city spoke to him, [saying]: Rabbi, the famous rabbi of theirs has come

held Hasidim to be heretics, as his claim proofs: "There is no forgiveness for heresy."[60] Afterwards, the *Gaon* left the city to not be in the same environment as Hasidim were.[61] There the *Gaon* heard that the Hasidim were valued with a revelation from Elijah for a new interpretation of the Zohar, he was even more outraged. Such revelations were only possible for selected individuals, and certainly no Hasidim,[62] as this was the peak and the *Gaon* was reassured in his suspicions and started with his campaign against the Hasidic sect and excommunicated Hasidim from Judaism, but he wanted everybody to see that Hasidim are not worthy.

In the lifetime of the *Gaon of Vilna*, his influence was too strong for a converging of the two groups, as Shneur Zalman states:

"Many years after the death of the Gaon he-Hasid of blessed memory, the merit of his Torah sustained him and all those who gathered in his shadow no longer to spill blood in vain, when it became evident in the eyes of all and the truth was known and seen clearly, that we have no hint of heresy, perish the thought, nor even a hint of a hint. For that reason the tribes were permitted to intermingle and the always intermarry with us, and likewise the other rejections and decrees, stringent and severe, of 5332 [1772] were annulled."[63]

One could conclude that after the death of the *Gaon* the relationships the Mitnaggdim and the Hasidim improved, though there was still the student

---

to debate with his venerable, holy Torah, and when he is defeated, certainly thereafter there will be peace upon Israel, he put them off with delays. And when they began to implore him greatly, he left and went away and traveled from the city, remaining there until our departure from the city." Citations taken from ibid., 80.

[60] Citation taken from ibid., 87.

[61] "And when the verdict against *morenu* Issar [a leader of Hasidim in Vilna] was issued, the Hasid [the Gaon] was not present here [in Vilna], but in Antikolya, and on Friday, before the holy sabbath, he assembled the leaders and was angry with them: Why have you been lenient in your judgment? If it depended on me, I would have done to them as Elijah the Prophet did to the Prophets of Ba'al. And the Hasid wished to place *morenu* Issar in the pillory, only the leaders did not desire that. And they struck him with a rubber whip in the kahal room before the welcoming of the Sabbath. And then they burned their writings before the pillory. And before 'He who dwells eternal,' he went up to the upper step, and the Hasidim, his comrades, stood at his right, ... and afterward they banned him. And all the week he sat in prison in jail of the citadel that they called 'Schloss.' And on the sabbath night he was held in the kahal room. [Emphasis in original.]" Citation taken from ibid., 89.

[62] Cf ibid., 82-83.

[63] Citation taken from ibid., 91.

of the *Gaon* – R. Hayyim of Volozhin. In his time of 'leadership' of Mit-naggdim the relations between Hasidim and Mitnaggdim took a different direction; as the Hasidim were recognized as well by the Russian Govern-ment. In Hayyim's time Hasidim were loathed because of their ideology or educational efforts, but they were not anymore excommunicated or perse-cuted.[64] According to Mitnaggdim the problem with Hasidism consisted in its approach to Torah study. Mitnaggdim did Torah study for its own sake, as *Torah lishmah*. In other words, for Mitnaggdim it was important and indispensable to remember and understand the content of the Torah in absolute contrast to Hasidim. Hasidim studied Torah for the sake to reach *dvekut* (communion with G-d), in theurgic ways. The *Besht*, for instance, underscored that prayer may be more important than the study of Torah. Heilman cites Martin Buber who emphasized that for Hasidim "the love of God is not to be attained by intellectual power or learning, but by the out-pouring of the soul in prayer."[65]

In other words Hayyim of Volozhin or Mitnaggdim tried to perpetuate the tradition of Torah study.[66] R. Hayyim was worried about the Torah degradation by the Hasidic approach, though he nevertheless appreciates the intention of Hasidim to reach G-d. However, he also had in mind that the Mitnaggdic way to Torah study as *Torah lishmah* is the primal reason for the world to be still intact. All prayers and keeping of *mitzvoth* are not worth as much as is Torah study. Nonetheless all Jews are responsible to keep the world alive by praying and observing the commandments.[67] In

---

[64] Cf ibid., 152.

[65] Citation taken from Heilman, *Defenders of the Faith - Inside Ultra-Orthodox Jewry*: 21.

[66] "I [R. Hayyim of Volozhin] also intended to write about the greatness of the obligation to deal with Torah, ... because it has been many days for Israel that occupation with the holy Torah has been laid low in every generation. And now, in these generations, it has fallen very very far, and it is placed in the obscurity of the lowest step, may the Merciful One save us. As our eyes see now that most of the sons our nation suffer greatly from bearing the burden of a livelihood, may God have mercy. And some of those who desire closeness to God have chosen for themselves to place the main em-phasis of their study in books of *yira* [fear of G-d] and ethics all the time, without placing the main burden of their occupation with the holy Torah in Scripture and in many Halakhot; ... may God forgive them, for their intention is for heaven, but this is not the way in which the light of the Torah dwells. [Emphasis in original.]" Citation taken from Etkes, *The Gaon of Vilna - The Man and His Image*: 164.

[67] "For even if, perish the thought, all the Jews lay aside and left off prayer to Him, may He be blessed, the worlds would not return to chaos because of that. Therefore, prayer is termed 'the life of the hour,' in the words of the Sages of blessed memory,

the end, the ice between Mitnaggdim and Hasidim thawed in the years to come, yes, a *rapprochement* was achieved; even if the main difference is still to locate to this day: the approach to the study of the Torah.

3. History and Theology of Hasidism

Much disturbance happened while and through New Hasidism gained foothold. First, the crisis with the failed messiah Shabbatai Zvi and Frankian messianic sectarian outcries did still reverberate, Mitnaggdim were right to feel pressure to preserve Judaism from the danger of Messianism. New Hasidism opposed the Mitnaggdim, because the new ones did estrange the Jewish masses in a certain way.[68]

In other words, mitnaggdic people were called *Hasidim* to highlight their piousness thus they studied, for instance, *Torah Lishmah*. The New Hasidim were, from their beginning on, regarded as a sect, which was named the New Pious ones.

Second, there was a crisis of Jewish self-government in Poland.[69] "The weakening of the leadership of the *kehillot* [Jewish communities] and the dispersal of the places of settlement in the provinces of Podolia and Volhynia apparently helped Hasidism to gain a foothold. [Emphasis in original.]"[70] One may ask why the New Hasidim gained success while Jewry in Eastern Europe was in a crisis. In a few words, the disciples of New Hasidism were able to reach the common folk and give them strength to believe in G-d.

The New Hasidim could enter the Jewish society with their kabbalistic approach, a kind of pious way, a *derechei hasidut*, and through their new way of religious practices.

---

whereas the Torah is called 'eternal life.' ... For the purpose of prayer is to add reparation in the worlds with the addition of sanctity at the time determined for them. Hence if the time has passed it will no longer be effective at all to continue giving an addition of sanctity and blessing in the worlds. However, the study of the holy Torah touches on the very vitality and existence of the worlds, lest they be entirely destroyed. Therefore a person must deal in it all the time always so as to erect and maintain the world at every moment." Citation taken from ibid., 177-78.

[68] Cf Harry M. Rabinowicz, *The World of Hasidism* (London: Vallentine, Mitchell, 1970). 9.

[69] Cf Benzion Dinur, "The Origins of Hasidism and Its Social and Messianic Foundations," in *Essential Papers on Hasidism - Origins to Present*, ed. Gershon David Hundert, *Essential Papers on Jewish Studies* (New York, London: The New York University Press, 1991), 87.

[70] Jakob Katz, *Tradition and Crisis - Jewish Society at the End of the Middle Ages* (New York: Schocken Books, 1974). 241.

All the practices and rituals, which seemed to be a new way or a new invention, were in fact scattered over the past centuries and is more a sort of collection by the New Hasidim.[71] It was a kind of renewal of Judaism.

But, in this time, it seemed to rock the established system, to be a danger to Jewish authorities. Especially the messianic danger was feared by them. It totally overshadowed their minds and therefore many Hasidim were excommunicated. However, it did not help to keep Hasidic preachers away from the Jewish flock. In contrast, they were unfazed and continued to act, to pray, and to preach to common Jews as usual.

The *Besht* was the founder of the movement Hasidism. He reformed Kabbalism in his way and put *dvekut* in the center of faith. He highlighted that Torah study must not be neglected, but mystical approaches were of higher significance; notwithstanding this, common Jews were also able to reach *dvekut*.

After the death of the *Besht*, R. Dov Ber (b. ? – d. 1772), the Maggid of Mezhirech, took over the 'movement' and consolidated it to a real movement, the New Hasidim;[72] – "If the Besht was the soul of Hasidism, the Maggid was its body."[73]

Not only these two persons laid the foundation stone of this young movement, there were several more. As we meet R. Shneur Zalman of Lyady (see below), or R. Yaaqov Yosef of Polonne, or The Maggid Rabbi Mendel of Bar, and the Maggid of Miedzyrzecz. I want to highlight with mentioning all these names that all of them created their own 'ideology' based on *Besht's* teaching.

The ideological part of Hasidim helps a lot to understand the new movement. As seen above, Hasidim tried to bring the Jewish folk closer to G-d with help of *derechei hasidut*. As the *Besht* once said, and which is still today one of the ideological points of Hasidism: "All have come into this world ... to show man how to live by three precepts: love of God, love of Israel and love of the Torah."[74]

Mitnaggdim taught Lurianic Kabbalah only themselves or were convinced that only a few ones were able to understand the Kabbalah. Hasidim, in contrast, did the absolute opposite and also taught average Jews.

---

[71] Cf Rachel Elior, *The Mystical Origins of Hasidism*, trans. Shalom Carmi (Oregon: The Littmann Library of Jewish Civilization, 1999). 99.

[72] Cf ibid., 85-94.

[73] Rabinowicz, *The World of Hasidism*: 43.

[74] Citation taken from ibid., 34.

One has to know that Hasidism approached the common people with its *Weltanschauung* of Lurianic Kabbalah and avoided to complicate this ideology, not like the pious (Hasidic, thus Mitnaggdic) Jewish leadership in Eastern Europe. Hasidim simplified the Kabbalistic approach by taking away the theological issues. The Kabbalistic thinking in Hasidism is in practice not a center of theosophy with all its complex theories. The center in this *Weltanschauung's* approach is the way to reach G-d in practical ways.

Hasidic rabbis prayed and learned for common Jews, who cared about their belief, and they got support via homilies. Hasidism became a movement in which people who could achieve *unio mystica* (partly achieved through *dvekut*) became not just mystics, but mystic leaders – the intention in mind to change the environment.[75] Keeping in mind the intention of Hasidim was to avoid a widening of the gap between rabbis and uneducated people.

"He [Jacob] was not praying only for his own sake, but for the entire people [in the time] of this last exile ... when hatred reigns between brothers and friends ... and their sin is remembered forever (like that of Esau [Esau is the synonym for the deadly foe of Jews]) ... 'I am afraid lest he come and strike me' – they, the rabbis, against the people, for strife has spread among the rabbis and among the people ... and this causes people as Esau, hoping to overcome his fellow."[76]

The danger feared by Hasidic preachers is an unbridgeable gap between rabbis and common Jews, which in consequence may lead to a worse situation. "When the people despise the scholars, then the Jews are forced to bend the knee to the unbelievers, and vice versa, the honor that they give to the scholars allows the Jews to transcend [the gentiles]."[77] The intention of this was to foster the relationship of scholars/rabbis and the common folk. R. Yaaqov Yosef described it as a body-soul connection: "The people who are called Jacob, they are the body, and the perfect faithful of Israel, who are called Israel, they are the soul."[78]

The element of faith in the *raison d'être* of Hasidism notwithstanding, they also sided with poor people, as Benzion Dinur claims. The Polish Jew-

---

[75] Cf Naftali Loewenthal, *Communicating the Infinite - The Emergence of Habad School* (Chicago: The University of Chicago Press, 1990). 3.

[76] Citation taken from Dinur, "The Origins of Hasidism and Its Social and Messianic Foundations," 146.

[77] Ibid.

[78] Citation taken from ibid., 153.

ish society was reigned by a few rich oligarchs, who did not care about the well-being of the Jewish underclass.[79] Hasidim entered this breach and thus they won sympathy in the folk.

The Hasidim came up with the idea to rely on their own ritual slaughter, *shechitah*. The Hasidim grabbed hold in Jewish society and had many followers, therefore many slaughters were needed. In consequence, the respective communities got no associated taxes from the unauthorized slaughters. Further Hasidim prayed separately; the communities, therefore, received no communal candle tax or synagogue tax, as it was usual at these times. And finally Hasidim did usually not support the local rabbi, because they had their own *Zaddik* (righteous person). "These and other similar social and economic elements caused deep communal resentment."[80]

To sum up, the *raison d'être* of early Hasidism consisted in an easy way of Lurianic Kabbalah. Hasidic preachers eased Lurianic Kabbalah by taking away theosophic argumentations in communication with common Jews or uneducated people, who were not able to read or had no time to read. By doing this the people could reach *dvekut* by listening or by prayer in Hasidic style. In the end, Hasidism got many followers, which led, as seen above, to economic penalties. Thus, the Jewish authorities were not only confronted with religious problems, but also with economic ones, which they did not expect and had to be fought, by excommunications, for instance.

The religious conviction of Hasidim contains mainly theosophically based parts. This means that Hasidim have a Kabbalistic related belief system. The first realm where the Hasidic theosophy shows itself is in the panentheistic area. "The whole earth is full of his glory."[81] In other words, G-d is omnipresent and immanent. This is not only based on the *Zohar*, it is also related to the *Midrash*; the Sages of Israel also claimed that G-d is the place, *ha-makom*. But one has to be very careful that this monistic Panentheism is not mixed up with Pantheism, which means that G-d is everything and thus a synonym with the universe. If this is taken as a fact, it would mean that G-d is good and bad, G-d is the sacred and the profane. How-

---

[79] Cf Rabinowicz, *The World of Hasidism*: 27.

[80] Cf Elior, *The Mystical Origins of Hasidism*: 102-03.

[81] Citation taken from Elijah Judah Schochet, *The Hasidic Movement and the Gaon of Vilna* (Northvale: Aronson 1994). 4.

ever, this "no place can be void of the Shekhinah"[82] ideology has to be understood from a different point of view. It means: evil is no longer an antithesis to good or an absence of G-dliness, but is a kind of a lower form of goodness or a divine spark encased in something evil.[83] In conclusion, Mitnaggdim did not understand the all-embracing Panentheism of Hasidism correctly. As it does not mean that G-d is everything, but that G-d is in everything and everything is of G-d as well, at least from the human angle. This is a difference which matters, because it is the difference between faith (Panentheism) and *apikursut* (heresy), Pantheism.[84] Panentheism is needed to back up everything in other theosophic parts in Hasidism.

One can also approach Hasidic Panentheism from a different angle. The man who laid the first bricks for the Habad movement, R. Dov Ber of Mezeritch, meant that through *dvekut* the person has to depict total *bitul* (self-abnegation), which is possible for all Hasidim. This is one step further in *unio mystica*; "the individual is described as no more than a hollow ram's horn through which the Divine breath blows."[85] R. Shneur Zalman of Lyady further elucidated this point by the demand that the *Kol Elohi* (Divine All) has to be the center of the consciousness: "there is nought apart from Him." In another situation, he put it quite similar:

"To sum up the matter: a person should be like someone who is not, with utter abandon of his body and soul, (as if) in order to be wiped out for the Sanctification of His blessed Name – from This World and The World to Come. ... Whether ... he was not born, or being born, is wiped out like an

---

[82] Gershom Scholem, "Devekut, or Communion with God," in *Essential Papers on Hasidism - Origins to Present*, ed. Gershon David Hundert, *Essential Papers on Jewish Studies* (New York, London: New York University Press, 1991), 281.

[83] Cf Schochet, *The Hasidic Movement and the Gaon of Vilna*: 66.

[84] Nevertheless, Pantheism remains in the Habad theosophy as well. Though, it is from a different point of view: It is from the G-dly point of view, as R. Aharon Halevi claims: "But as for the Infinite in Its blessed essence, everything is one, aside from which there is nothing, and there is nothing beside Him and nothing beyond Him and truly everything is His power. However this power is utterly inconceivable. Therefore all things may be endlessly divided. Nevertheless there will be in Him neither plurality nor change." Citation taken from Rachel Elior, *The Paradoxical Ascent to God - The Kabbalistic Theosophy of Habad Hasidism*, trans. Jeffrey M. Green (Albany: State University of New York, 1993). 60-61. Therefore everything that seems to exist is nothing at all, besides the divine substance or divine essence which gives life to it. Cf ibid., 61.

[85] Loewenthal, *Communicating the Infinite - The Emergence of Habad School*: 3.

animal. ... As far as he is concerned he is already completely annihilated, due to gazing at the greatness of the Creator."

Panentheism is in this approach, in other words, described as a not-being in achieving in the process of *unio mystica*, the absolute selfabnegation – as one has never been, as is explained by this Panentheism, because of the declaration of not-being and admitting that only G-d and singly G-d is.

The *Mitteler Rebbe* or namesake of R. Dov Ber of Mezeritch, R. Dov Ber also dedicated Panentheism a paragraph to:

"And this is the main aim in all contemplation of whatever detail, throughout the downchaining (of the worlds), from before the first Veiling (Zimzum) to the lowest level of the realm of Action – that everything should be (perceived as) absorbed in the simple Unity which is the Essence of the radiance of the Infinite [*Ein Sof*]."[86]

This paragraph means that it does not matter if you are, it does matter to accept that you are not being. Through the acceptance of this fact you have to bring the higher sphere (thus G-dly sphere) to the lower sphere (the, as it seems, humanly sphere) through contemplation through all *sfirot*[87] to unite the Single Unity as it is.

Dvekut[88] is the major theosophic part in Hasidism, because it centers the religious *raison d'être* of Hasidism and shows the orientation of Hasidim to common Jews.

Dvekut has its roots in Kabbalistic doctrine of the Middle Ages. Nahmanides, a well-known exegete, was influenced by Kabbalism in the 13th century. He wrote about *dvekut* that of "those who abandon the affairs of this world and pay no regard to this world at all, as though they were not corporeal beings, but all their intent and purpose is fixed on their creator alone, as in the cases of Elijah and Enoch, who live forever in body and soul, after having attained Communion of their souls with the Great

---

[86] Citations taken from ibid., 3, 40-41, 153.

[87] Sfira (sg.) – vessel. It is meant to explain that G-d manifested H-mself in ten vessels on earth, but only in an abstract kabbalistic-esoteric understanding.

[88] "HASHEM, your God, shall you follow and Him shall you fear; His commandments shall you observe and to His voice shall you hearken; Him shall you serve and *to Him shall you cleave*. [Emphasis added.]" Deut. 13:5, Irving Stone and Helen Stone, eds., *Tanach - The Stone Edition* (New York, Bnei Brak: Mesorah Publications, 2000).

Name."[89] Though, as Scholem argues, to understand Hasidic *dvekut* one has to know the commentary on Deuteronomy 11:22[90] of Nahmanides:

"It warns man not worship God and somebody beside Him; he is to worship God alone in his heart and his actions. And it is plausible that the meaning of 'cleaving' is to remember God and His love constantly, not to divert your thought from Him in all your earthly doings. *Such a man may be talking to other people, but his heart is not with them since he is in the presence of God.* And it is further plausible that those who have attained this rank, *do, even in their earthly life, partake of the eternal life,* because they have made themselves a dwelling place of the Shekhinah [last *sfira* of the ten *sfirot* in Kabbalah, female part of G-d]. [Emphasis in original.]"[91]

One has to pay special attention to the earthly actions of men while being in communion with G-d. This part was taken over by the *Besht* who used it for his teachings. Yisrael Baal Shem Tov gave an interesting explanation of why one has to reach *dvekut*:

"When a father teaches his young son how to walk, what does he do? He places the child on his feet and reaches out with his arm sot hat [sic!] the child will not fall down. As the child toddles between teh [sic!] father's arms, the father moves backward bit by bit, and the child follows. The more the father moves back, the harder the child tries to reach him. That's how he learns to walk.

God acts toward man in the same manner. When a Jew passionately seeks communion with God, God responds by distancing Himself. This only intensifies the Jew's yearning. The more detached from God the Jew feels, the strong is his longing to be near Him."[92]

According to the *Besht* it is obligatory to reach *dvekut*.

In other words, one has to be in *dvekut* all the time, if one does not negate G-d. "The Baal Shem formulated it in the words of the Torah (Deut. 11:16), *ve-sartem-va-avadtem elohim aherim,* 'lest you turn aside and serve other gods,' meaning, 'once a man turns aside from *devekut* and the fixation of his

---

[89] Citation taken from Scholem, "Devekut, or Communion with God," 275.

[90] "To love the Lord your God, to walk in all His ways and to cleave unto Him." Carroll and Pricket, *The Bible - Authorized King James Version with Apocrypha.*

[91] Citation taken from Scholem, "Devekut, or Communion with God," 277.

[92] Citation taken from Neal Walters, "Good Shabbos everyone," Amerisoft Inc., http://www.amerisoftinc.com/wwwboard/messages/76.html. [17/01/2012].

thought on God, he is considered as one who serves other gods and there is no mediating path.' [Emphasis in original.]"[93]

Of course the all-time-being of *dvekut* was a trigger for the Mitnaggdim, because the Besht and his circle claimed that it was more important to be in communion with G-d than *Torah Lishmah*. For example R. Menahem Mendel of Peremyshlyan states:

"And there is one more principle: not to study a great deal, for in the First Generation when they had powerful minds ... they did not need to trouble themselves about Reverence, as Reverence was constantly present to them and they were able to study a great deal. But we, who have weaker minds, if we let our thoughts drift from their *dvekut* with God Blessed Be He and study a great deal, Heaven forbid we may stop thinking about the Reverence of God. ... Therefore, one should limit one's study and constantly thinking of the greatness of the Creator. ... And not think many thoughts in one's mind, but only the one thought. [Emphasis in original.]"[94]

"This thesis aroused considerable hostility and was quoted in all polemical writings against the [Hasidic] movement as a proof of its subversive and anti-rabbinic tendencies."[95]

But the originality of Hasidism is the way to reach *dvekut*, to reach G-d, through the preachers who teach the public[96] or to reach H-m personally with headstands or similar approaches. Gershom Scholem endorses that it is just the faith in G-d which is enough to reach *dvekut*.[97] In absolute contrast stand the pious ones (the Mitnaggdim) who approach H-m with theosophic arguments or reach G-d with theoretical approaches of *Torah Lishmah*.

How to study the Torah correctly? This question was, is, and will probably remain the most discussed, disputed, and influential characteristic of Hasidism, and the presumed falseness in this matter in the eyes of Mitnaggdim was responsible for the excommunication of Hasidim as they were mainly confronted with the accusation to consciously neglect the Torah study by their preference for other mystical approaches. Thus the *Gaon*

---

[93] Scholem, "Devekut, or Communion with God," 281.

[94] Citation taken from Immanuel Etkes, *The Besht - Magician, Mystic, and Leader,* trans. Saadya Sternberg (Hanover, London: University Press of New England, 2005). 122.

[95] Scholem, "Devekut, or Communion with God," 279.

[96] Cf Gershom Scholem, "Die jüdische Mystik in ihren Hauptströmungen," (Sinzheim: Suhrkamp Taschenbuch Verlag, 1967), 375.

[97] Cf Scholem, "Devekut, or Communion with God," 280.

of Vilna was concerned and demanded *a fortiori Torah Lishmah*, the study of the Torah for its own sake, as it is in his view the main priority for a Jew.

Hasidim, in contrast, put the Torah study just as one of several possibilities as obligations for a Jew. In other words, Hasidim take the study of Torah into consideration, yes, they study the Torah. But it is not their main intention to study the Torah for its own sake, but for higher motives, as for instance the achievement of *dvekut*.[98] *Torah Lishmah* notwithstanding remains a pillar in the theology of Hasidism. The Alter Rebbe, R. Shneur Zalman wrote that one can study the Torah as *Shelo Lishmah* (not for the sake of its own), but one willy-nilly ends to study *Torah Lishmah*.[99]

Rabbi Shneur Zalman once told Rabbi Joshua Zeitlin: "The Hasidim, too, set aside time for study. The difference between them and the *Mitnagdim* is this: the latter set time for study and they are limited by a time factor, whereas the former make the Torah their path of life. [Emphasis in original.]"[100] In other words, Hasidim showed the common people that the Torah is important, but does not need to be studied at fixed hours. However, with the help of the Torah the simple man can reach *dvekut*.[101]

The *Besht* himself taught it in this way. A man who studies the Torah "must study the Torah to become a Torah."[102] It is possible to connect Panentheism and Torah study. Thus R. Shneur Zalman went a similar way

---

[98] Cf Etkes, *The Besht - Magician, Mystic, and Leader*: 120.

[99] "However, when a person is engaged (in service) truly not for its own sake, but for some personal motive, with a view to his own glorification, as, for example, in order to become a scholar, and the like, then that motive, which originates in the kelipat nogah [shining shells, as it may be used in self-interest], clothes itself in his Torah, and the Torah is temporarily in a state of exile in the kelipah [shell], until he repents, since '(Repentance) brings healing to the world.' For with his return to G-d, his Torah also returns with him. Therefore the Rabbis of blessed memory declared, 'A man should always occupy himself (with Torah and precepts, even if not for its own sake), for from motives of self-interest he will come (to study and observe) for its own sake' — (this they state) with certainty, for ultimately he is bound to do repentance, whether in this incarnation or in another, 'Because none is rejected by Him.'" R. Schneur Zalman of Lyady, "Likutei Amarim - Chapter 39," Kehot Publication Society, http://www.chabad.org/library/tanya/tanya_cdo/aid/1029067/jewish/Chapter-39.htm. [06/17/2012].

[100] Citation taken from Rabinowicz, *The World of Hasidism*: 75.

[101] Cf ibid.

[102] Citation taken from ibid., 38.

as the *Besht* and said that the Holy One and the Torah are one.[103] The Torah has to be understood as an intermediary, which brings the higher spheres (the letters of the Torah are seen as holy) to the lower spheres, some unveiled by *Zimzum* (contraction) flowing as Divine Radiance to the human spheres. This opportunity of union can be fulfilled through recital or study of the Torah, even if one is not able to recognize it, based on the fact of the physicality of the text or the practical action. "It is like one who embraces the King. It makes no difference to his closeness and cleaving to the King whether he embraces Him when He is wearing one robe or several robes – since the body of the King is within."[104]

A good summary of the Hasidic idea of the Torah may be a quote of R. Shneur Zalman. "My soul desired Torah, so I set out for Vilna [stronghold of the Mitnaggdim]. But, on the way, I changed my mind. A little knowledge of the Torah I had already acquired, but of the principle of true worship I had yet learned nothing. I needed a guide who would show me how to serve God."[105] He found this guide in R. Dov Ber, the Maggid of Mezeritch. In other words, for Hasidim the practice of prayer was as important as the theory in the knowledge of Torah, therefore the Torah study was not conducted with the same intention with which the Mitnaggdim approached it.

These were all in all the main reasons how Hasidism could set a foot in the threshold of Eastern European Jewry. Not only the intention the Hasidim gave to the low class of Jewry, but as well the Hasidic way of theosophy, with *dvekut* as its practical center, put them into the center of Eastern European Judaism. Their theosophic approach was not messianic. The *Weltanschauung* of Hasidim was a new way, the *derechei hasidut*.

---

[103] "When a person occupies himself in the Torah, his neshamah, which is his divine soul, with her two innermost garments only, namely the power of speech and thought, are absorbed in the Divine light of the blessed [*Ein Sof*], and are united with it in a perfect union."

R. Schneur Zalman of Lyady, "Likutei Amarim Chapter 35," Kehot Publication Society, http://www.chabad.org/library/tanya/tanya_cdo/aid/1029034/jewish/Chapter-35.htm. [06/17/2012].

[104] Citation taken from Loewenthal, *Communicating the Infinite - The Emergence of Habad School*: 88.

[105] Citation taken from Rabinowicz, *The World of Hasidism*: 68.

4. The Habad movement in its History and Theology

The next pages should serve as a kind of introduction to the Habad movement. I will highlight the historical development, and will afterwards take a look at the complex theology of the movement.

The movement was founded after the death of several of the founders of the *New Hasidim*, including the *Besht* and Dov Ber, the Maggid of Mezeritch. The first man/Rebbe and Zaddik[106] of the Habad movement was R. Schneur Zalman (b. 1745 – d. 1813), in Lyady in today's White Russia.

R. Schneur Zalman's ideology is represented in his book *Tanya*[107] which is still used as a guideline. In a few words, his ideology is "that [it] integrated intellectualism and scholarship with the values of spirituality, faith, and simplicity."[108] In R. Schneur Zalman's lifetime the movement could spread over Belarus and was widely accepted in Jewish communities in this country. "The distinction, however, between the purely ideological elements within the early movement and the social orientation that accompanied its expansion are difficult, today, to separate from each other."[109] Therefore it is not of importance to further discuss the early struggles of the

---

[106] "The *Zaddik* is conceived as [a person who reaches] for the highest level of esoteric attainment, with the concomitant aim to employ this power for the benefit of others. The teachings of the Baal Shem Tov and the Maggid [two *Zaddikim*] showed the methods to be employed, particularly during prayer, by means of which the *Zaddik* could purify and elevate the world. [Emphasis in original.]" Loewenthal, *Communicating the Infinite - The Emergence of Habad School*: 39.

[107] The book Tanya "acts both as a body of teaching for intellectual study and also as a manual of guidance for spiritual striving. ... The *Tanya* ... seeks to map out a variety of paths, some suitable for the man of stature with pneumatic [spiritual] power, other for the rational scholar. ... The Tanya intended to provide the advice its author would have given face to face in the heightened atmosphere of the *Yehidut* [personal meetings with the Rebbe] situation. 'All of (the teachings in the book) are answers to many questions which the members of our fraternity [the Habad movement] in this region ask continually, each one on his own level, seeking advice in Divine service. For there is no longer enough time to answer each person's question individually; also, forgetfulness is common. Therefore I [R. Shneur Zalman] have written down all the answers to all the questions, so that each person should have a permanent record and will no longer have to strive to speak to men in *Yehidut*.' [Emphasis in original.]" Ibid., 47-48.

[108] Mark Avrum Ehrlich, *Leadership in the HaBaD Movement - A critical Evaluation of HaBaD Leadership, History, and Succession - with Particular Emphasis on Menachem Mendel Schneerson* (Northvale: Aronson, 2000). 11.

[109] Ibid., 128-29.

movement, as it is only important to know that it was successful with its teaching in its beginnings.

After the death of R. Schneur Zalman his son R. Dov Ber (b. 1773 – d. 1827), the *Mitteler Rebbe*, took over the leadership and moved the headquarters to Lubavitch; there was a short-lived split up of the movement, which were to be found Lubavitch, Lyady, and Kapost. Though, today the only true successor is the movement, which was moved from Lyady to Lubavitch.

The qualities of R. Dov Ber were to observe, in contrast to his competitors, his scholastic experience about ecstasy. Further, he was a descendant of R. Schneur Zalman and an effective communicator, which was a most important factor and stood in the center of the good communication scheme of the movement. R. Dov Ber's strategy consisted mainly in teaching the masses the ideas of his father, but he used his father's fame to his own advantage. He proofed to be a good successor, as not only the biological reason spoke for him, but also the ability to reach the masses, which leads one to come to this conclusion. [110]

After the death of R. Dov Ber his son-in-law and the grandson of R. Zalman, R. Menachem Mendel Shachna (b. 1789 – d. 1866), named *Zemah Zedek,* succeeded him. "His youth and subsequent longevity made his leadership one of the most successful in HaBaD history; his hasidim numbered in their millions."[111] The *Zemah Zedek* was a scholar, who was known for his excellent knowledge in halakhic and mystical questions. His accomplishments were twofold, there were the good relations with Mitnaggdim, because of the common enemies: first, the *Haskalah,* which got stronger in Eastern Europe, and, second, the Russian government, and there was the uniting of the movement with the split-up of Staroselye.

Zemah Zedek's sixth son R. Shmuel (b. 1834 – d. 1883) was his successor. R. Shmuel reigned the Habad movement for 16 years, as can be seen in the transformation of the Habad philosophy to let more *Rebbeinim* preach and by becoming universalistic, as the philosophy did reach many places.[112]

The *Fifth Rebbe* was R. Shalom Dov Ber (b. 1860 – d. 1920), a son of R. Shmuel, who finally cemented that leadership in the Habad movement moves from father to son. R. Shalom Dov Ber got famous for his far reaching influences, seen in his frequent travelling and prolifically writing to

---

[110] Cf ibid., 170-87.
[111] Ibid., 194.
[112] Cf ibid., 194-231.

various places in Russia, Europe, and the United States. Further, he established relations with other Hasidic and many Jewish leaders. "His political activism brought him to an awareness of the essential challenges to Eastern European Jewry in general, and to the Habad movement in particular. His exposure to the ideas of socialism and Zionism made him familiar with their ideological temptations. He actively sought solutions to what he considered the erosion of Judaism and of the Habad movement."[113] R. Shalom Dov Ber demanded more affiliation to his Habad movement, therefore an own yeshiva, *Tomchei Temimim* (supporters of the pure ones) was established – an important step in the history of the Habad movement; it brought not only Hasidim back to the Habad movement, but also the messianic meaning given to the yeshiva by the Rebbe Dov Ber. "He declared that this institution had a divine mission that would hasten the messianic arrival."[114] Regarding this the Rebbe clarified that he disliked Zionism and criticized the orthodox party *Agudat Yisrael*, too. "He argued that the messianic redemption was first and foremost a mystical process and could not be achieved by force or political ventures."[115] The Rebbe Dov Ber relocated the movement's headquarters from Lubavitch to Rostov in 1915 and eventually transformed it into a 'universal Jewish mission.'[116] R. Dov Ber was one of the important *Rebbeinim* of the Habad movement, as he did reign for a long time in sometimes challenging episodes; for instance the upcoming of the Soviet Regime and many pogroms against Jews.

The *Sixth Rebbe*, Rebbe Yosef Yitzchak (b. 1880 – d. 1950), took over the position as Rebbe immediately after the death of his father. In his lifetime, the religious life for Jews in Europe was very difficult. This Rebbe became famous in the whole world for his fight for Jews in Russia – he was a member of the Rabbinic Council which was confronted with the problem of many rabbis leaving Russia. The Rebbe also took over the leading position in the Council. His reputation was rather based on being politically, socially, and publicly active than being a scholar.

In 1927, he was imprisoned by the Soviet Regime and sentenced to death, as he had already been spied on by the Regime since he had taken over of the Rabbinic Council. However, the sentence was repealed due to international pressure, as "his status was compared to that of the Pope or a

---

[113] Ibid., 244.
[114] Ibid., 245.
[115] Ibid.
[116] Cf ibid., 236-46.

head of a religious hierarchy."[117] In his lifetime the headquarters of the movement often changed its locations and ended up in New York. Thereto fled the Rebbe Yosef Yitzchak in 1940, where the headquarters are still located. He there established, inter alia, the political organization *Agudat Hasidei Habad* (Union of Habad Hasidim), which worked alongside *Anshei Habad* (People of Hasidim) that had already been established in 1924. The afore mentioned was thought to renew the Habad Hasidic consciousness in the United States, but it helped *a fortiori* as an instrument for the Habad movement around the world.[118]

The Rebbe Yosef Yitzchak lived at the times of the foundation of State of Israel. He went to this country, which was called *Eretz ha-Kodesh* (the holy land) by the Habad people, to establish a village for Habad, Kfar Habad, in 1949. In 1950 the Sixth Rebbe died, but he was not declared for dead, because he had proclaimed that the Messiah would come in his lifetime. His successor *the Rebbe* Menachem Mendel Schneerson was sure about this and *the Rebbe* stated that R. Yosef Yitzchak "would emerge as the *mashiah* [messiah] and that in fact, he was not dead at all."[119]

The Rebbe Menachem Mendel Schneerson took over the position as Rebbe in 1951, as he was the son-in-law of the dead predecessor. *The Rebbe* made the Habad movement into the probably best known Jewish organization around the world. He reformed it to a strand which is located in countries where otherwise no Jews resided. His ideas in connection with modernity were highly discussed, but he finally became famous and respected for this. After all he was the undisputed ruler of the movement and seen by many as the Messiah, but he died at the age of 92 in 1994, since then no new Rebbe has come into sight.[120]

Habad is an acronym, which consists of three words: *Hokhmah* (wisdom), *Binah* (understanding), and *Daat* (knowledge). These three words are the three highest *sfirot* in the Kabbalistic system of divine emanation.

It has foremost to be clarified what the meaning of the acronym Habad is in theological matters, then I will touch upon the broader theology of the movement. "*Hokhmah* represents the creation in its earliest potentiality: the idea of a finite world as it is first born in the divine mind. *Binah* is the idea conceived in its details, the result of contemplation. *Daat* is, as it were, the

---

[117] Ibid., 267.
[118] Cf ibid., 252-83.
[119] Ibid., 116.
[120] Cf ibid., 11-14.

commitment to creation, the stage in which the idea becomes an active intention. [Emphasis in original.]"[121]

This means that G-d needed the world to be perfect, seen in *Hokhmah*. In *Binah*, thus, G-d created the world in H-s 'mind' and finally shaped it, in *Daat*. Habad gave this Kabbalistic description a further meaning, so that it also describes the inner life of a human being out of the logic that "the human soul is a microcosm of the universe, and its workings reflect the process of cosmic creation."[122] In other words, every human being, especially a Jew, is able to locate G-d within her/his own human soul, therefore the human actions are seen by H-m and therefore it is of the highest importance to fulfill the *mitzvoth*. Thus every Jew or, in this context, member of the Habad movement needs to study and meditate to find G-d in himself. It is interesting that the Torah study gets a new importance in the level of reading the Torah in a *Hasidut*-way. It means to read the Torah to find not only the essence of the Torah and the universe, but also of someone's own soul.[123]

One further has to take into consideration that the Habad movement does missionary work. In other words, they try to convert as many Jews as possible to their belief of Judaism in order to bring as many Jews as possible to the level to be able to find G-d in themselves. The Habad movement sees itself and all other Jews as the Chosen Ones by G-d, "destined to play a unique role in the messianic redemption of creation."[124] This justifies their missionary activity; all Jews have to find their 'G-dly' soul, *nefesh elokhit*, to be able to connect with G-d and by doing this hasten redemption. This soul is the theological justification of belonging to the Chosen Ones, because this soul contains a spark of the *Or Ein Sof*, Light of Infinity, which is able to connect with G-d. He Himself connects with the sparks through *Hokhmah*, the *sfira*.[125]

This G-dly soul, *nefesh elokhit*, exists in every Jew, but every Jew also has the animal soul, *nefesh bahamit*, which also every gentile has. This difference plays an important role for the Habad adherents in the understanding of

---

[121] Tzvi Rabinowicz, "Habad," in *The Encyclopedia of Hasidism* (Northvale: Aronson, 1996), 161.

[122] Ibid.

[123] Cf ibid., 161-62.

[124] Cf Henry Goldschmidt, "Religion, Reductionism, and the Godly Soul: Lubavitch Hasidic Jewishness and the Limits of Classificatory Thought," *Journal of the American Academy of Religion* 77, no. 3 (2009): 553.

[125] Cf ibid., 554-55.

humanity, social life, and politics, because gentiles and Jews with their *nefesh bahamit* are mainly motivated to act selfishly, hedonistically, and to please the worldly desires and act as if there were outside of reality. In other words, the animal souls in human beings are limited to the reality as it appears to men. In absolute contrast to people with an active *nefesh elokhit* which bends itself 'instinctively' toward the will of G-d. This concludes in an activity bound on unselfish morality. Thus it will be followed willy-nilly by a fulfillment of all *mitzvoth*.[126]

R. Shneur Zalman wrote in *Tanya* about it and it serves as a perfect example:

"The neshamah [G-dly soul or *nefesh elokhit*] of man ... naturally desire and yearn to separate itself and depart from the body in order to unite with its origin and source in G-d [achieve *dvekut*], the fountain-head of all life, blessed be He, though thereby it would become null and void, completely losing its entity therein, with nothing remaining of its former essence and being [achieve the absolute selfabnegation, *bitul*]. Nevertheless, this is its will and desire by its nature. [see below] ... This nature stems from the faculty of [*Hokhmah*] found in the soul, wherein abides the light of the blessed [*Ein Sof* – this represents the Infinite; see below]."[127]

This paragraph means that the G-dly soul wants to depart from the body (to depart from reality) to bring the Higher Spheres (this represents the Infinite/*Ein Sof*) down to earth through a connection with *dvekut* or if possible with *bitul*. This is the desire of nature, because this also is G-d, as will be seen below. The nature as explained in the citation comes from *Hokhmah*, because of the fact that in every human being an image of the creation of the world by G-d can be found. This activates the *nefesh elokhit* to force Herself to break with nature, even if it is also G-d, to bring down or rise to Higher Spheres (to G-d, who is as well called *Ein Sof* or the Infinite (the absolute naught – not imaginable for any human being). One can illustrate this with another paragraph which concentrates more on contemplation in order to achieve the descent of the Higher Spheres, which is the will of G-d.

"The world and all that fills it dissolved out of existence in relation to its source, which is the light of the blessed [Ein Sof]. When one will deeply contemplate this, his [the Jew's] heart will be gladdened and his soul will

---

[126] Cf ibid., 556.

[127] R. Schneur Zalman of Lyady, "Likutei Amarim - Chapter 19," Kehot Publication Society, http://www.chabad.org/library/tanya/tanya_cdo/aid/1028943/jewish/-Chapter-19.htm. [06/18/2012].

rejoice even with joy and singing, with all heart and soul and might, in (the intensity of) this faith which is tremendous, since this is the (experience of the) very proximity of G-d, and it is the whole (purpose) of man and the goal of his creation [of the human creation], as well as of the creation of all the worlds, both upper and lower, that He [G-d] may have an abode here below."[128]

In a few words, one has to achieve *dvekut* or *bitul* and reach the communion with the Higher Spheres and it is now possible to be in a state of being in the Higher Spheres or bring down the Higher Spheres at the same time (!) to fulfill G-d's wish.

As the explanation for the paradox has to follow – it must be said that the *nefesh bahamit* is also a part of G-d, in a paradoxical meaning. In other words, the animal soul is existent in everyone, as well as there is the G-dly soul in every Jew. The *nefesh bahamit* shows the *Yesh*, the existence, the material world, but one can only know G-d, if one is able to be aware of the *nefesh elokhit*. Simply put the *nefesh elokhit* is something like the naught, *Ayin* or *Ein Sof*. Both *Yesh* and *Ayin* are G-d. The meaning is paradox, because the *Yesh* is in the world and the *Ayin* comes into the world, thus both are there. The world is created by G-d and H- is both *Yesh* and *Ayin*. One has to conclude that according to the Habad knowledge – there is nothing beside G-d;[129] the world is H-m but not H-m, too.[130] In other words, it is *Acosmism*, the idea of G-d with nothing besides H-m.[131]

---

[128] R. Schneur Zalman of Lyady, "Likutei Amarim Chapter 33," Kehut Publication Society, http://www.chabad.org/library/tanya/tanya_cdo/aid/7912/jewish/Chapter-33.htm. [06/18/2012].

[129] Dt. 4:35: "Unto thee it was shewed, that thou mightiest know that the Lord he is God; there is none else beside him." Carroll and Pricket, *The Bible - Authorized King James Version with Apocrypha*.

[130] Cf Elior, *The Paradoxical Ascent to God - The Kabbalistic Theosophy of Habad Hasidism*: 103-08.

[131] "For when the intellect in the rational soul deeply contemplates and immerses itself exceedingly in the greatness of G-d, how He fills all worlds and encompasses all worlds, and in the presence of Whom everything is considered as nothing." R. Schneur Zalman of Lyady, "Likutei Amarim Chapter 3," Kehot Publication Society, http://www.chabad.org/library/tanya/tanya_cdo/aid/1028876/jewish/Chapter-3.htm. [06/18/2012]. A further proof is seen in the words of Maimonides. He wrote in *Mishneh Torah, The Book of Knowledge* about the existence of G-d and the fact of nothing besides H-m. "The basic principle of all basic principles ... is to realize that there is a First Being who brought every existing thing into being. ... If, however, it were supposed that all other beings were non-existent, He alone would still exist.

In summation, the theology of the Habad movement is very complex, but I tried to simplify it. The Habad adherents believe in two souls – *nefesh elokhit* and *nefesh bahamit*, which are both found in Jews. Though, the *nefesh elokhit* has to be found by every Jew through Torah study, by achievement of *dvekut* or *bitul*, thus one proceeded even further, to connect the Higher Spheres with the Lower Spheres in both ways by bringing down the Higher to the Lower and by ascending the Lower to the Higher, at the same time. If case of success it is possible to bring the existence *Yesh* and the naught *Ayin* together, but it is paradox; nevertheless, one has to know that there is nothing besides G-d, therefore G-d is both *Yesh* and *Ayin*.

5. Excursus: Messianism

In each topic I discuss Messianism will always play a part. It is obvious to observe in the behavior of the Habad movement – as their latest leader *the Rebbe* Menachem Mendel Schneerson was seen by many of his followers as the up-coming Messiah. He disseminated much Messianism during his ruling of the Habad movement.

Gershom Scholem distinguishes between two different variants of Messianism: firstly, the restorative Messianism, and secondly, the utopian-catastrophic Messianism. The meaning of the restorative one is that the Jews will be brought back to their original state, thus they will return to a political sovereignty, as it was in existence in the kingdom of David. In other words, the Jews would close the circle of history and would be able to perform all the commandments.

In absolute contrast to the before mentioned Messianism is the utopian version, also called apocalypticism, as an entirely new world will be created. It is totally different from any versions human beings can imagine; maybe it is related to the *Gan Eden* (Paradise). This messianic version will happen in a sudden rupture.[132]

Their non-existence would not involve His non-existence. ... That is what the prophet means when he says 'But the Eternal is the true God' (Jer. 10:10); that is, *He alone is real*, and nothing else has reality like His reality. The same thought the Torah expresses in the text: 'There is none else besides Him' (Deut. 4:35); that is: *There is no being besides Him*, that is really like Him. [Emphasis added.]" Maimonides, *Mishneh Torah - The Book of Knowledge*, trans. Moses Hyamson (Jerusalem: Boys Town Jerusalem Publishers, 1965). 34a.

[132] Cf David Biale, "Gershom Scholem on Jewish Messianism," in *Essential Papers on Messianic Movements and Personalities in Jewish History*, ed. Marc Saperstein, *Essential Papers on Jewish Studies* (New York, London: New York University Press, 1992), 522.

As I discussed above the paradox theology of the Habad movement, the question of how Messianic tendencies fit in this complex theology arises. But, if the Habad adherents reach their *nefesh elokhit* through Torah study, one can suppose that they reach a *dvekut*, too. In this time one will be able to locate the Messiah, because then it is possible to come to a different time counting. In the chronology it is not possible to locate the time at one single point, therefore one has to leave the chronology and take the single point of time as given. There is the past, the present, and the future in one single point of time – as *the Rebbe* Menachem Mendel Schneerson said: "immediately and without delay in actuality."[133] At this point the Messiah is already located. Yet one has to reach this with one's personal *nefesh elokhit* with *dvekut* or better *bitul* and then it will be possible to see the Messiah.[134] This is only the theory, in practice nothing like this happened though that one could see the Messiah, though *the Rebbe* himself was declared to be the Messiah.

After his death, the Habad movement broke into two strands. One side proclaimed that the Rebbe is the Messiah, the other negated it. The Habad movement, which represents mainly the declared non-Messianists, cited that Maimonides explained the obligations a would-be Messiah has to fulfill:

"If we see a Jewish leader who (a) toils in the study of Torah and is meticulous about the observance of the mitzvot, (b) influences the Jews to follow the ways of the Torah and (c) wages the 'battles of God' — such a person is the 'presumptive Moshiach.'

If the person succeeded in all these endeavors, and then rebuilds the Holy Temple in Jerusalem and facilitates the ingathering of the Jews to the Land of Israel — then we are certain that he is the Moshiach."[135]

The obligations fulfilled by the Rebbe, are (a) to (c). He looked for a meticulous observance of the commandments. He influenced many Jews to follow the ways of the Torah, by, for instance, establishing the *'Mitzvah*

---

133 Citation taken from Eliot R. Wolfson, *Open Secret - Postmessianic Messianism and the Mystical Revision of Menahem Mendel Schneerson* (New York: Columbia University Press, 2009). 278.

134 Cf ibid., 278-80.

135 unknown, "Who is Moshiach? - The Basics," Moshiach 101, http://www.chabad.-org/library/moshiach/article_cdo/aid/1121893/jewish/The-Basics.htm. [06/19/20-12].

Tanks'[136] or by sending *Shilhot* (Habadic emissaries) to the farthest corners of the earth. The battles of G-d were led by *the Rebbe* as well. But *the Rebbe* did neither reach the building of the Third Temple, nor was he able to gather the Jews for redemption – as one has to understand the phrase – to the Land of Israel. All in all, *the Rebbe* had potential in the eyes of non-Messianists of the Habad movement, but he was not the Messiah. He was only seen, by them, as the 'Son of Josef,' who dies, and then the Messiah, the 'Son of David,' may come.[137]

There are so-called Schneersonists whose beliefs are contrary to the non-Messianists' one. They believe that *the Rebbe* is the Messiah and will soon come back from the dead. Though, we locate similarities to Early Christianity, who went the exact same way. The Messiah Jesus died and after a while he came back from the dead. "Schneersonism is growing closer to Christianity and distancing itself from Judaism – why – because Judaism has no place for messiah or the worship of a dead man."[138] There are still many Habadniks and rabbis who believe that *the Rebbe* is the Messiah, but for this discussion another paper would be necessary.

---

[136] "The Rebbe, Rabbi Menachem Mendel Schneerson, of righteous memory, had sent his tanks into the battle for the soul of the American Jew. If a large part of American Jewry had ceased to come to shul [synagogue] each morning to don *tefillin* [phylacteries] and pray, the Rebbe was going to bring the *tefillin* to them. He was going to send one of his students to stop the American Jew on a city sidewalk. 'Excuse me, sir,' the lad would say. 'Are you Jewish?' If the answer is affirmative, the young man would continue: 'Would you like to put on tefillin today? It's a mitzvah.' The American Jew will be invited to step up onto the truck, roll up his left sleeve, bind the tefillin to his arm and head and recite a short prayer. [Emphasis in Original.]"
unknown, "1974: The Mitzvah Tank," Chabad-Lubavitch Media Center, http://www.-chabad.org/therebbe/timeline_cdo/aid/62178/jewish/1974-The-Mitzvah-Tank.-htm. [06/19/2012].

[137] "The rabbis have taught; The Holy One, blessed be He, will say to Messiah ben David [Son of David], may he be revealed soon in our day!; 'Ask if Me anything, and I shall give it to you, for it is written, The Lord said unto me, Thou art my son, this day have I begotten thee, ask of Me and I will give the nations for thy inheritance (Psalms 2:7-8)' And when he will see that Messiah ben Joseph [Son of Josef] will be slain, he will say before Him: 'Master of the World! I ask nothing of you except life! God will say to him: 'Even before you said, 'life,' your father David prophesied about you as it is written, He asked life of the, Thou gavest it him (Ps. 21:5)." Babylonian Talmud Sukkah 52a unknown, "The Messiah of Judaism," Truthnet.org, http://www.tru-thnet.org/TheMessiah/4_Messiah_of_Judaism/. [06/19/2012].

[138] Shelomo Alfassa, "Lubavitch's Break-Away Religion of 'Schneersonism' is Growing," Shelomo Alfassa, http://alfassa.com/schneersonism.html. [06/19/2012].

In summation, there is a tendency of Messianism in the Habad movement and the belief in the coming of the Messiah (not who the actual Messiah will be) is used to bolster almost every argument. The Habad movement relates itself more to the first description of the possible redemption by Scholem. They believe that redemption will be related more on the Halakhic rules than on anything unknown, thus restorative Messianism.[139]

---

[139] Cf Tzvi Freeman, "Tradition or Progress," Chabad, http://www.chabad.org/library/article_cdo/aid/269549/jewish/Tradition-or-Progress.htm. [06/19/2012].

Chapter II: Habad in the State of Israel

1. 'Who is a Jew?'-Debate

After the foundation of the State of Israel the government had to pass a bill about a right to 'return' as a Jew to the Jewish state of Israel. In fact the 'right to return' was given to every Jew on the whole globe, as stated in the first paragraph of the *Law of Return*: "1. Every Jew has the right to come to this country [Israel] as an oleh [immigrating Jew to Israel]."[1] The intention of this law was not only to provide the newly founded state with potential citizens. Behind the *Law of Return* stood rather the idea to guarantee an automatic Israeli citizenship to Jews that they would not be forced to wander in the world or be stateless, especially after the cruelties of the Shoa.[2] Among the national-religious oriented public a lively debate about the *Law of Return* arose. It was questioned by the National Religious Party (NRP) in the late 1950s, to be quite exact in 1958. The NRP resigned collectively from the government in the third Knesset as they were disappointed by the instructions of Israel Ben-Yehuda, the Interior Minister. He decided that new immigrants to Israel should be treated in good faith – immigrants did not have to prove their belief. The proposal of the NRP to decide the 'Who is a Jew?' question in accordance with the explanation of the Halakhah was not implemented.[3] Prime Minister David Ben-Gurion asked several known Jewish scholars by way of mail what they thought about the matter of 'Who is a Jew?' question.[4]

This letter was intended to receive answers for current problems in the State of Israel; as for instance the registration of children of mixed mar-

---

[1] Israeli-Government, "Law of Return," Israel Ministry of Foreign Affairs, http://www.mfa.gov.il/MFA/MFAArchive/1950_1959/Law+of+Return+5710-1950.htm. [04/21/2012].

[2] Cf Daniel Sinclair, "Halakhah and Israel," in *Modern Judaism - An Oxford Guide*, ed. Miri Freud-Kandel and Nicholas Robert Michael De. Lange (Oxford, New York: Oxford University Press, 2008), 356.

[3] unknown, "The Law of Return - Implementation Cases," Jewish Agency, http://www.jewishagency.org/JewishAgency/English/Jewish+Education/Compelling+Content/Eye+on+Israel/Activities+and+Programming/Law+of+Return/7.+The+Law+of+Return++Implementation+Cases.htm. [05/01/2012].

[4] See Eliezer Ben-Rafael, *Jewish Identities - Fifty Intelllectuals Answer Ben Gurion* (Kiryat Sede-Boqer: Ham Merkaz Le Moreset Ben Gurion, 2001).

riages with a gentile mother, who did not convert. Furthermore, Ben-Gurion worried about security issues – he thought about identity cards, in which the religious denomination, also labeled 'ethnic community,' and the 'nationality', that means if she/he is Jewish, in comparison to Arab, were mentioned. "In his guidelines, Ben-Gurion asks for an answer that will fit in with tradition as accepted by all Jewish groups, by all streams of both orthodox and liberal Judaism, as well as Israel's special situation as a sovereign Jewish state guaranteeing the freedom of conscience and religion and as the center for the ingathering of the exiles."[5] Nevertheless, the Prime Minister insisted "Israel's legislation prohibits discrimination between individuals on the basis of differences of race, color, nationality, religion, or sex."[6] Ben-Gurion received 46 replies, and 38 of them "recommended that the State [of Israel] apply the halachic criteria."[7] The only consequence for the moment was the withdrawal of the Minister of the Interior and the Attorney-General[8] "after new elections [had] enabled Ben-Gurion to install in the interior ministry a National Religious Party minister who immediately rescinded his predecessor's regulations."[9]

The first time the *Law of Return* was seriously questioned in its content and implementation is the Rufeisen/Brother Daniel Case. Oswald Rufeisen was born as a Jew, but converted to Christianity in 1942 to secure himself in the Holocaust, and then even accepted Roman Catholicism wholeheartedly. He became a monk in 1945 and wanted to immigrate to Israel in this position. He claimed that he wanted to be accredited as a Jew, as he had been born by a Jewish mother and as this was in accordance with the Halakhah, and that therefore he had the right to take advantage of the *Law of Return*. In other words, he wanted to remain in his catholic faith, but his nationality should be Jewish. In fact his position was strengthened by the Chief Rabbi of Israel who confirmed that Brother Daniel had to be considered as Jewish.[10] The Supreme Court, nevertheless, decided that it was not possible for apostates to be regarded as Jewish in nationality, if they volun-

---

[5] unknown, "The Law of Return - Implementation Cases". [05/03/2012].

[6] Ibid. [05/03/2012].

[7] Landau, *Piety and Power - The World of Jewish Fundamentalism*: 294.

[8] Cf unknown, "The Law of Return - Implementation Cases". [05/03/2012].

[9] Landau, *Piety and Power - The World of Jewish Fundamentalism*: 294.

[10] Cf Barbara Weill, "Summary of Definitions on Who is a Jew?," Jewish Agency for Israel, http://www.jafi.org.il/JewishAgency/English/Jewish+Education/Compelling+Content/Eye+on+Israel/Activities+and+Programming/Israel-Achieve/Summary+of+Definitions+on+Who+is+a+Jew.htm. [04/30/2012].

tarily decided to convert to another religion. Judge Berensohn explained the Supreme Court's decision with the following words: "It is a serious application and the applicant is proud of his Jewish affiliations; but for the people, an apostate has dissociated himself from the religion, the people and the community of Israel. The same person cannot be both Jewish and Christian."[11]

The case in other words, the *Law of Return* was applied only to Jews, who were born by a Jewish mother, as it is written in the Halakhah, and if the applicant is not a member of a different faith – as Brother Daniel, however, was. Notwithstanding, Brother Daniel could reside in Israel, not in application of the *Law of Return*, but in the naturalization procedure – one has to remain for five years in Israel to become a citizen. However, Brother Daniel wanted to raise the question of the use of the *Law of Return* in principle, for whom it is valid and for whom not. The Supreme Court in the State of Israel for the first time faced the question to have to give a legal description of Jewishness – is it a nationality or is it a religion, initially it was both.[12] In reaction to the Brother Daniel case the Ministry of the Interior published new regulations in 1960. In these stated that an individual who is registered "as a Jew by 'religion' and 'nationality' must be Jewish according to halacha and [...] must not practice another religion."[13] The ultra-Orthodox Jews became more interested in the discussion about the *Law of Return* and the definition of a Jew in the State of Israel. *The Rebbe* had already set his opinion about the state of Israel and the halakhic concerns. He negated the possibility of a Jewish State of Israel for him she was only a State of Jews.[14]

---

[11] unknown, "The Oswald Rufeisen / Brother Daniel Case Court Summations," Jewish Agency, http://www.jewishagency.org/JewishAgency/English/Jewish+Education-/Compelling+Content/Eye+on+Israel/Activities+and+Programming/Law+of+-Return/19.+THE+OSWALD+RUFEISEN.htm. [05/01/2012].

[12] Cf Rabinovich and Reinharz, *Israel in the Middle East - Documents and Readings on Society, Politics, and Foreign Relations, Pre-1948 to the Present,* 173.

[13] unknown, "Testing the Principals," Anti Defamation League, http://www.adl.-org/israel/conversion/testing-principles.asp. [05/04/2012].

[14] "A machine, system, etc., can be used at different degrees of efficiency, for a small job or a big maximum job. The State of Israel can be a State of Jews -- another Levantine State, as Syria is the State of Syrians, or it can become something exceptional, unique, namely a Jewish State. But to be a Jewish State it must be run according to the Jewish Torah and tradition. This is not a contradiction to its being a 'normal' State with men, women and children, institutions, etc. as any other. But only in this way will it be a Jewish State, exceptional."

In 1970 the next case, with a lot of public attention, took place in Israel: "Commander [Benjamin] Shalit, a Jewish, non-believing navy officer born in Israel, married a non-Jewish, Scottish woman. When the registration offices refused his request to register his two children as Jewish, he appealed in 1970 to the Supreme Court which supported his claim, and ruled that according to the Law of Return, his children were to be registered as belonging to the Jewish ethnic community."[15] The case was of importance, as the children were not born by a Jewish mother and therefore in regard of the Halakhah are not Jewish. The Supreme Court, however, decided in favor of the claimant. As the Court mentioned once again, the judges are not obligated to rely on the Halakah, but they decide solely for the State of Israel and the well-being of her citizens – it was a secular decision and not based on religious reasons. It is impossible to understand the situation without more background knowledge.

It was common practice to register the offspring of gentile wives of Jews who emigrated from Europe to Israel as Jews in the categories 'religion' and 'nationality,' even if it was halakhically not correct. When marrying, as demanded by the religious parties in the government, Jews, who were born by a Jewish mother, should marry according to an orthodox practice. Other Jews, though, who were halakhically not Jewish should marry according to the Halakhah; nevertheless, the respective rabbinate was to decide on these issues. Benjamin Shalit, however, married his wife, a gentile, outside of Israel (*huz laaretz*). In Israel, Shalit's wife gave birth to two children, who were automatically recognized as Israeli citizens. The case was only taken to the Supreme Court, because Shalit demanded, as the couple was atheistic, that nationality should be registered as Jewish and the religion part should be left blank. The Interior Ministry refused his claim and wanted to leave both parts blank, neither nationality nor religion should be called Jewish. The case went on as mentioned above; in the judgment the Court stated explicitly that "it is in fact a mistake to think that the matter under consideration requires us to determine who is a Jew."[16] Finally, the Ministry of Interior was forced to change its registration policies and called the

---

Interview with the Rebbe Rebbe Menachem Mendel Schneerson, "The Rebbe Speaks to Hillel Students," Chabad, http://www.chabad.org/therebbe/article_cdo/-aid/392177/jewish/The-Rebbe-Speaks-to-Hillel-Students.htm. [06/19/2012].

[15] Weill, "Summary of Definitions on Who is a Jew?". [05/03/2012].

[16] unknown, "Testing the Principals". [05/04/2012].

Knesset to pass an amendment of the *Law of Return*. This was the beginning of a heated debate between religious and *hiloni* Israelis (secular Jews).[17]

The first amendment was presumably in accordance with the religious populace. It was an amendment to section 4B of the *Law of Return*: "For the purposes of this Law [of Return], 'Jew' means a person who was born of a Jewish mother or has become converted to Judaism and who is not a member of another religion."[18] The second amendment of the *Law of Return*, however, was not completely in a halakhic manner; as section 4A states: "The rights of a Jew under this Law and the rights of an oleh [immigrant] under the Nationality Law [of 1952] as well as the rights of an oleh under any other enactment, are also vested in a child and a grandchild of a Jew, the spouse of a Jew, the spouse of a child of a Jew and the spouse of a grandchild of a Jew, except for a person who has been a Jew and has voluntarily changed his religion."[19] In consequence the *Population Registry Law* was also amended in 1970 and was passed by the initiation of the NRP. The new law decreed "that individuals registering as Jew by 'religion' or 'nationality' must be a 'person who was born of a Jewish mother or who has converted to Judaism.'"[20] In effect the Shalits could not register their third child as a Jew. The Supreme Court also denied their request.[21] This produced not only problems for the Shalit family. One has to know that tens of thousands of gentiles from the former Soviet Union were affected by this oddity. On the one hand, they had the right to immigrate under the *Law of Return*, but on the other hand, they could not be registered as Jews. As the immigrants were neither born by a Jewish mother nor converted to Judaism, they could not marry Jews or be buried in a Jewish cemetery as a consequence of the contradiction between the *Law of Return* and the *Population Registry Law*.

Furthermore, the amendment to the *Law of Return* was not out of discussion, as it did not define the way of conversion to Judaism. This led to a series of additional cases in the next decades.

Nevertheless, the Supreme Court declared that every gentile, who converted to Judaism in the Diaspora with a legal attestation of their Jewish faith, has to be credited to immigrate to Israel under the *Law of Return*. This

---

[17] Cf Sinclair, "Halakhah and Israel," 356.
[18] Israeli-Government, "Law of Return". [05/05/2012].
[19] Ibid. [05/05/2012].
[20] unknown, "Testing the Principals". [05/05/2012].
[21] Cf ibid. [05/05/2012].

ran counter to the demands of the orthodox parties, which tried to force the Knesset to change the *Law of Return* by a new amendment – this should declare that new converted Jews shall only convert in an orthodox way to get the right to immigrate to Israel under the *Law of Return*. "The court followed the secular approach to Jewish identity for citizenship purposes established in earlier decisions. It also followed the principle of international law according to which certificates in matters of personal status issued by other countries, including certificates of conversion to Judaism, must be accepted at their face value unless patently false."[22]

We meet another oddity in Israeli law. On the one hand, one can convert to Judaism in diasporic countries (*huz laaretz*) into any denomination of Judaism. This contradicts, on the other hand, the inside-Israeli way of conversion. In the State of Israel conversions to Judaism have to be approved by the Chief Rabbinate, which is an orthodox institution deriving its authority from a law introduced in the year 1925, at the time of the British Mandate.

The Begin government and the orthodox parties, the NRP and *Agudat Yisrael*, jointly tried to amend the *Law of Return* by inserting a requirement for want-to-be-Jews to convert under orthodox rulings. Notwithstanding this bid having failed, it produced an aftershock in the diaspora communities, especially in the Reform and Conservative Jewish denominations of North America, because if the orthodox conversion procedure of Begin and his orthodox coalition partners had worked, it would have brought the other Jewish believers into factual de-legitimation.

Shoshana Miller, an American who converted to Judaism under the auspices of a Reform Rabbi, immigrated to Israel in 1985 under the *Law of Return*. Miller's *aliyah* (immigration) application was passed, as a case similar to Miller's had already been dealt with in the law of 1970. However, she did not receive an identity card which identified her as a Jew, because she did not convert under Orthodox rulings. She directly went to the Supreme Court, supported by the *Movement for Progressive Judaism* and the *Association of Reform Zionists of America*. The Court instructed the Ministry of Interior to give her an identity card; the reaction of the Minister of Interior, Yitzhak Peretz, however, was a compromise – Peretz recommended that all converts would get an identity card stating they were proselytes. This compromise was unanimously rejected by the Supreme Court as it would

---

[22] Sinclair, "Halakhah and Israel," 357.

create two Jewish peoples; it would even "run counter to the national aspirations for which the state was established."[23]

Shoshana Miller, withal, left Israel a few days after the Court decision, but her case created a precedent that at least furnished the Supreme Court with a guideline. The next non-orthodox proselytes who wanted to get an identity card identifying them as Jews were remitted by the Ministry of Interior, until the Supreme Court decided in reference to the Miller Case that it is not allowed to put off the applications any longer. Gail Moscowitz, an American, and Julia and Claudio Varella, a couple from Brazil, were the first non-Orthodox converts who received identity cards with a reference to their Jewish status on them.

In conclusion to all these oddities between the *Law of Return* in reference to converts and the *Population Registry Law*, the Supreme Court decided to prohibit further questionings of the status of *olim* (immigrants) in relation to their Judaism. The Ministry of Interior is only allowed to ask the applicant for further proofs of her/his Jewishness.[24]

This peculiar fight, however, between Orthodox and secular people in Israel was not over yet. The next episode was to take place in 1990. The Brazilian Hava Goldstein immigrated to Israel and converted to Judaism under Reform auspices in Israel a year later. In *huz laaretz* she married an Israeli Jew born in Brazil. The fact of being a Jew gave her the right to apply for Israeli citizenship. Her entry into Israel was passed, but her registration as a Jew in the Interior Ministry was denied. The Ministry demanded a proof of her Jewishness. Once again, the Supreme Court was called upon. It granted the Interior Ministry six months for the registration of Goldstein.[25] It is necessary to repeat that conversion in Israel had to take place under the auspices of an Orthodox institution as the Chief Rabbinate only recognized conversions based on the 1925 Mandatory Ordinance in Israel.[26]

The Supreme Court recognized their far reaching decision, but refused to be responsible for further incidents, as the President of the Supreme Court, Judge Barak, stated:

"We have decided that in order to recognize conversion pursuant to the *Law of Return* and the *Population Registry Law*, it need not comply with the

---

[23] unknown, "Testing the Principals". [05/07/2012].

[24] Cf ibid. [05/07/2012].

[25] Cf unknown, "The Conversion Crisis 1995 - Present," Anti Defamation League, http://www.adl.org/israel/conversion/crisis.asp#4. [05/07/2012].

[26] Cf Sinclair, "Halakhah and Israel," 357.

requirements of the 1925 Ordinance. We are not taking this matter any further. We are not deciding which conversion is valid under these two laws. We are also not deciding whether a Reform conversion is valid pursuant to the *Law of Return* ... Hence we have not ordered that the petitioner be recognized as Jewish under the *Law of Return*, and we have not ordered that she should be registered as Jewish in the Population Registry. [Emphasis in original.]"[27]

After all, the Supreme Court limited its scope only to the abilities of the Ordinance of 1925. In the non-judicial world the Reform and Conservative Jews hoped that the Labor Government, *in persona* Prime Minister Shimon Peres, would allow non-Orthodox conversions in Israel. It was not Peres who disappointed the non-Orthodox Jews; it was his Interior Minister Haim Ramon, who said "that he would not support the registration of Goldstein as a Jew both as a matter of principle and of political survival."[28] The next government, under Binyamin Netanyahu, had beside the NRP also Shas as an Orthodox coalition partner in 1996. Their coalition agreement stated: "The law of conversion shall be changed so that conversions to Judaism in Israel will be recognized only if authorized by the Chief Rabbinate." In other words, this was a step into the direction of an *'Orthodoxation'* of Israel. Netanyahu, though, said that any non-orthodox conversion *huz laaretz* will still be recognized in Israel – as demanded by the Supreme Court.

For the proposal of the new law of conversion, the Netanyahu government came up with an idea to formulate guidelines for non-Orthodox conversions which should be accepted by the non-Orthodox Jewish communities, for instance, the Reform and the Conservative movements. Netanyahu founded a committee under the chairmanship of Yaakov Ne'eman. Ne'eman, a well-known lawyer, was to bring the representatives of the Orthodox, the Reform, and the Conservative movements to an agreement. Together they should find a solution to the conversion procedure. More than thrice the deadline for the committee was extended. But after more than fifty meetings in more than seven months Ne'eman submitted a report to Netanyahu in January 1997. The Ne'eman committee formulated a guideline for all three movements. The preamble of their proposal declared:

---

[27] Citation taken from ibid., 358.
[28] unknown, "The Conversion Crisis 1995 - Present". [05/08/2012].

"It is agreed by all parties that there must be a single, uniform, official conversion procedure that will be conducted in accordance with Jewish law and will be recognized by all segments of the Jewish people. ... The composition of the commission, which includes representatives of both the Reform and Conservative movements, reflects a desire for cooperation among all three major movements in Judaism and for Jewish unity."[29]

In fact, this program worked. 'Conversion institutes' were developed, who were run by different denominations and financed by the *Jewish Agency*. The Orthodox Jews can proceed with their own conversions, as these are always very strict, but the Reform and Conservative movement agreed to terminate with their conversion procedures outside the institutes. From then on all converts enjoy an additional advantage, as they were immediately recognized as Jews by the state and the Chief Rabbinate. In other words, for the first time non-Orthodox conversions in Israel were accepted as valid by the Chief Rabbinate.

The label in the identity card, which signifies the person's status should be exchanged against a *yud* (which may be taken as *Yisraeli* or *Yehudi* (Jew)), is marked with an additional date. For born Jews it is the birth date and for proselytes it is the day of conversion.[30]

To give the discussion a pretended full picture, I cite two further incidents. In the Beresford case the Supreme Court had to decide whether so called messianic Jews were allowed to immigrate under the *Law of Return*. Messianic Jews are Jews who believe that Jesus is the Messiah. In effect, the Supreme Court came to the conclusion that this version of Judaism does not fit the secular definition of Jewishness in Israel, therefore this kind of Judaism is not allowed to immigrate to Israel under the *Law of Return*.[31] In a similar matter the Chief Rabbinate of Israel did not accept a convert to Judaism who converted to the Messianic strand of the Habad movement. The Rabbinate claimed that they do not accept one as a Jew, if he claims that *the Rebbe* is the Messiah.[32]

Though, there is an article in *Haaretz* that disagrees with all the above mentioned positive results for non-Orthodox conversions. Yair Ettinger

---

[29] Ibid. [05/08/2012].
[30] Cf ibid. [05/08/2012].
[31] Cf Sinclair, "Halakhah and Israel," 357.
[32] Cf Shmarya Rosenberg, "Rabbi David Berger - Shmuley Boteach 'Wrong'," Shmarya Rosenberg, http://failedmessiah.typepad.com/failed_messiahcom/2008/01/rabbi-david-ber.html. [06/19/2012].

wrote on December 19th 2011 that the Chief Rabbinate is the sole institution to decide in matters of foreign conversions, if the respective person is considered a Jew. The Interior Ministry of Israel gives the Chief Rabbinate the authority to be in charge of applications of immigration under the *Law of Return*. The problem is not the Chief Rabbinate and its decisions, the problem is that many proselytes, even if they converted under orthodox auspices, are not regarded as Jews, because of the fact that the respective rabbi does not belong to an accepted denomination or accepted organization of rabbis. This is in fact contrary to a plethora of judgments of the Supreme Court.[33]

The whole description of the discussion about the matter of 'Who is a Jew?' is supposed to explain how difficult it is for a Jewish state to define its own potential citizens.[34] Though, it is presumably the case that the ultra-Orthodox faction disagrees with the solution which was found in the end. But how did the Habad movement react and take part in this discussion? In the following part I try to cover the positions of the Habad movement.

The first time the Habad movement was in fact confronted with the question to define a Jew was when Prime Minister Ben-Gurion wrote a letter to *the Rebbe* and asked him for his personal opinion about the 'Who is a Jew?' question. The Rebbe answered as follows:

"My opinion is absolutely clear, in conformity with the Torah and the tradition accepted for generations, that in these matters there can be no validity whatsoever to a verbal declaration expressing [one's] desire to register as a Jew. Such a declaration has no power to change the reality.

---

[33] Cf Yair Ettinger, "Israel Interior Ministry still letting Chief Rabbinate decide 'who is a Jew'" Haaretz, http://www.haaretz.com/print-edition/news/israel-interior-mini-stry-still-letting-chief-rabbinate-decide-who-is-a-jew-1.402198. [05/23/2012].

[34] Nevertheless, even today the State of Israel representatives still do not know how to define their state as *Jewish*, even though they represent it. Mostly these persons only demand it, but are not going into more into detail, as one article in *Haaretz* suggests. See Joel Braunold, "What is a 'Jewish State'?," Haaretz, http://www.haaretz.-com/jewish-world/what-is-a-jewish-state-1.415908. [05/16/2012]. Though, it is as well a liberal immigration law for Jews. At least Haredim are not excited about this law. See Mordecai Plaut, "Should Non-Jews 'Return' under the Law of Return?," Chareidi.org, http://www.chareidi.org/ATCOTU/snjrutlor.html. [05/16/2012]. In fact, there are various opinions in the non-orthodox world about being a Jew or not being a Jew. A very interesting article appeared in *Haaretz*: See Marc D. Angel, "Torah can be used to let new Jews in, not keep them out," Haaretz, http://www.ha-aretz.com/opinion/torah-can-be-used-to-let-new-jews-in-not-keep-them-out-1.432080. [05/24/2012].

According to the Torah and the tradition of ages which still exists today, a Jew is only a person born of a Jewish mother, or a proselyte who has been converted in conformity with the exact procedure laid down in the authoritative codes of Judaism dating to ancient times. This applies not only to children whose parents or guardians declare their desire to register as Jews, but whoever declares his or her wish to enter the Jewish community. I do not cite sources, since there are clear and detailed rulings on the matter."[35]

When reading of differing sources one gets the impression that the Habad movement is really concerned about the 'Who is a Jew?' debate. *The Rebbe* was able raising ire with his hawkish position in the Secular and the Reform Movement in the United States.[36] Menachem Friedman sees different-ent reasons for the concern of the Habad movement for the question of 'Who is a Jew?' in Israel. Friedman sees it related to the *Tefillin* campaign, as discussed below. The *Tefillin* campaign sets Jews apart from gentiles or the Jews' non-Jewish surroundings; therefore the Jew gets purer, or holier. This happens only, though, if this is accomplished by a Jew who is one according to the Halakhah. Therefore, he has to be born of a Jewish mother or has converted in a legitimate orthodox way. Otherwise, if one is a non-legitimate convert, it would be an anti-Messianic move.[37] The Habad movement wanted to have a halakhic version of a definition of a Jew in a law in Israel, as one can see especially in the statement by *the Rebbe* I cited above. Nevertheless, I elaborate this in detail to better illustrate the con-cerns of the Habad movement.

R. Jacob Immanuel Schochet, a well-known member in the Habad movement, provides a whole pamphlet on the question of 'Who is a Jew?' in English.[38] He published a revised issue after the Knesset elections in

---

[35] Citation taken from Edward Hoffman, *Despite All Odds - The Story of Lubavitch* (New York: Simon and Schuster, 1991). 171.

[36] Cf Ehrlich, *The Messiah of Brooklyn - Understanding Lubavitch Hasidism Past and Present*: 98.

[37] Cf Menachem Friedman, "Habad as Messianic Fundamentalism - From Local Particularism to Universal Jewish Mission," in *Accounting For Fundamentalisms - The Dynamic Character of Movements*, ed. Martin E. Marty and R. Scott Appleby (Chicago, London: The University of Chicago Press, 1994), 350-51.

[38] There is a Hebrew pamphlet written by *the Rebbe*. See Rebbe Menachem Mendel Schneerson, *About the Question: Who is a Jew and about Converts in a Halakhic Commentary.*

1988.[39] In this pamphlet R. Schochet explains in detail why it is important to significantly amend the *Law of Return*, adding that only an orthodox conversion is valid,[40] as it strictly follows the halakhic way.[41] I cover the most important statements of R. Schochet and connect them to the mentioned discussion and, afterwards, compare them to the meaning of Jewishness in the theology of Habad.

R. Schochet sees a '*Greuel-Propaganda*' (horror propaganda) campaign set against the orthodox demands of a correction of the *Law of Return*. The rabbi writes that arguments were raised; an orthodox attempt to fight all other Jewish movements; to amend the *Law of Return* is the same as to delegitimize all non-Orthodox Jews; Israel will not be a safe haven for Jewish refugees anymore, if the Law will changed; it is an artificial discussion by the Orthodox Jews; it is a purely religious problem that has to be removed from the political agenda; and the sole way to preserve the Jewish unity is to keep the *Law of Return* as it is.[42] This cannot be true, since otherwise he would not have written this book in the way he did. "Its sole purpose was, and remains, to teach, to clarify, to reason, and to reaffirm the fundamental principles of 'justice, truth and peace.' As such it forges an inviolable bond between the author and all those who share these ideals."[43]

If one reads the pamphlet of R. Schochet carefully, one stumbles over a lot of simplifications. The first simplification is Schochet's definition of a 'Jew.' He offers three possible ways to define the Jew: race, nationality, or

---

[39] The elections for the Israeli Knesset in 1988 were very successful for the Haredi parties. All Haredi parties together with the NRP won 18 of 120 seats. In the forming of a coalition the NRP, *Agudat Yisrael*, *Shas*, and *Degal Ha-Torah* were involved. Therefore, "the haredi parties, together with the [NRP], now demanded that the Law of Return be amended by adding to the Law's definition of a Jew – 'a person born by a Jewish mother or converted to Judaism' – the three words 'according to halacha'. The Lubavitch movement spearheaded the campaign, lobbying vigorously in the Knesset corridors and mounting a major advertising effort in the media." Landau, *Piety and Power - The World of Jewish Fundamentalism*: 316.

[40] This is supported by Reuven P. Bulka, a modern-Orthodox Rabbi from Ottawa, Canada. "It would be ridiculous for Reform rabbis to insist that converts be holier than they ... By Orthodox standards, a Reform conversion is an exercise in futility, and the convert is, by Orthodox standards, as non-Jewish as before." Citation taken from ibid., 298.

[41] Cf R. Jacob Immanuel Schochet, "Who is a Jew? 30 Questions and Answers About This Controversial and Divisive Issue," http://www.whoisajew.com/. [05/12/2012].

[42] Cf ibid. [05/12/2012].

[43] Ibid. [05/12/2012].

religion. Race and nationality are out of question for him, as for the afore-said one it is impossible since there are too many different Jews: "Yet there are Jews of every race and color: black and white, oriental and Occidental. Descendants of every conceivable race have joined the Jewish people throughout the ages."[44] The next one, nationality, is impossible as well: "Nationality can hardly be a definition for a people that has been dispersed throughout the world for close to two thousand years, without a country or homeland of its own. For about two thirds of the years of its existence, the Jewish people lived among different nations: Egyptians and Babylonians; ... Germany; Poland; ... etc."[45] Therefore, religion remains the only possible definition. Jewish faith is the only character that distinguishes a Jew from a gentile.[46] This belief 'exclusively' relates Jews to the Land of Israel. "If not for the Bible, if not for the religious aspects and obligations relating the Jews and the Land of Israel, there would be no bond whatsoever between

---

[44] Ibid. [05/12/2012].

[45] Ibid. [05/12/2012].

[46] This is substantiated by Nissan Mindel, *The Divine Commandments*, 11th ed. (New York: Kehot Publication Society, 1945). 19.

As Mindel states: "The relationship between Israel and G-d through the medium of our religion is explained in the *Zohar* as follows: 'Three are interlocked together: (the people) Israel, the Torah and the Holy One, blessed be He, and all are on different planes, one higher than the other, partly hidden, partly exposed.' [Zohar III, 73a]

The meaning of this saying is that the three – Israel, the Torah and G-d – are linked to-gether like a chain of three rings, of which the upper part of the bottom ring is held by the lower part of the middle ring, and the upper part of the middle ring is held by the lower part of the top ring.

In each of the three rings there is a hidden part and a disclosed part. Similarly are appar-ent qualities and latent qualities in each of the three: Israel, the Torah and G-d. ...

The manner of their union is twofold:

The revealed qualities of Israel unite with the revealed attributes of G-d by means of the revealed part of the Torah; and the latent qualities of Israel unite with the latent at-tributes of G-d by means of the latent part of the Torah;

The revealed qualities of Israel are connected with the hidden qualities of Israel, and the hidden qualities of Israel in turn unite with the revealed part of the Torah; the re-vealed part of the Torah is connected with its esoteric part, and this in turn unites with the revealed attributes of G-d; finally, the revealed attributes of G-d are con-nected with His hidden attributes and thus the union is completed.

It follows therefore that **this union with G-d is extant in every one of Israel**, man or woman, young or old, **whether learned in the Torah or ignorant of it**. [Bold empha-sis added, italic emphasis in original.]"

the People of Israel and the Land of Israel."[47] In consequence, everyone, who was part of the original covenant, which was contracted between G-d and the Jews, plus the proselytes joining over the centuries and all their descendants, are Jews.[48] One could ask R. Schochet, how Jews cannot be a 'race,' to use the rabbi's own words, if today's Jews are descendants from Jews of thousands of years ago. R. Schochet asked himself the question and answered as follows:

"Without contradicting our definition of jewishness [sic!] ... there is, then, a 'racial-ethnic-nationalist' aspect to Jewish identity as well. It differs though from the normative definition of racial or nationalist identity. The latter is usually understood in terms of a common source of genetic or geographic origin, and/or common physical features. Quite obviously this does not apply to any definition of Jewish identity. The 'racial,' 'ethnic' or 'nationalist' aspect of Judaism and Jewishness, and the 'common denominator' shared by all Jews, is based on, established, and defined exclusively by the religious criteria: the religious premises of Judaism determine who is a Jew, what constitutes Jewish 'race,' and how we define Jewish nationalism."[49]

In consequence, people can even 'convert' to other beliefs, but they remain Jews and, therefore, are obligated to the Torah. Further, it is, as the Halakhah announces, only matrilineal descent. R. Schochet concludes that there are either Jews or non-Jews.[50] This is in concord with *the Rebbe*:

"The rational soul (which is the matter of the divine image) in the Jew is not comparable to the rational soul in the Gentile ... for the rational soul of the Jew is in a manner different than the rational soul in the human species ... for Israel is called 'sons of God,' as they have a divine soul, and thus their rational soul is also in another manner than the rational soul in the human species. And the principle difference between them is that the intellect of the divine soul is humble ... it can attain nullification, which is not so in the intellect of the world (the rational soul) that effectuates being ... and it can lead to arrogance ... when it acquires an intellectual matter."[51]

---

[47] Schochet, "Who is a Jew? 30 Questions and Answers About This Controversial and Divisive Issue". [05/12/2012].

[48] Cf ibid. [05/12/2012].

[49] Ibid. [05/12/2012].

[50] Cf ibid. [05/12/2012].

[51] Citation taken from Wolfson, *Open Secret - Postmessianic Messianism and the Mystical Revision of Menahem Mendel Schneerson*: 239.

Therefore Brother Daniel could have immigrated under the *Law of Return*, though all of Shalit's children would have remained non-Jewish.

In the next argument, R. Schochet explains how one has to convert to Judaism. Primarily, one has to accept the principles, the teachings, and the practices of Judaism. Secondly, one has to be circumcised and immersed in a *mikveh* (a ritual pool) when male or when female, only immersed in a *mikveh*. All this has to be supervised and guided by authorized representatives. In this context by Orthodox rabbis who are qualified for such conversion procedures. Such a *dayan*, a judge, can only be a rabbi who believes in and is committed to all traditions of Israel and observes all laws and statutes of the faith. In other words, the *dayan* has to know the *Shulchan Aruch* (written by R. Yosef Caro (b. 1488 – d. 1575) in 1555), the code of Jewish Religious Law, which is of highest importance in the theology of the Habad movement and also in several other ultra-Orthodox communities. "Under the halacha, conversion requires three conditions, administered by a beit din [court with *dayanim* as judges]: immersion in a ritual bath, circumcision for males, and 'acceptance of the yoke of the commandments' – in Hebrew, *tevila, mila,* and *kabbalat ol mitzvot*. [Emphasis in original.]"[52] By this explanation, R. Schochet does not explicitly exclude all rabbis who are not in the Orthodox practice and, as is cleared later on, does exclude these rabbis who do not believe in every detail of the Halakhah or adapted it to modernity. In other words, as R. Schochet explains, the rabbis of the 'conservative' or 'reform' movement, for instance, do not have the qualities as the *Shulchan Aruch* demands, as these rabbis do disagree with the 'immutability' of Torah-laws. Therefore, "it is self-evidently absurd, and altogether unacceptable, to appoint as a representative of the Jewish faith someone who denies all or a part of that faith."[53] In part 17 of his pamphlet, R. Schochet states that conversions can only be valid, if they are conducted in accordance with this *Shulchan Aruch*. Therefore, all conversions, which were not done according to Orthodox rulings, but nevertheless accepted in Israel, are not valid in R. Schochet's opinion. In consequence, the conversions done by the institutes of conversion, led by the Reform movement or the Conservative movement, are invalid.

R. Schochet delves deeper and explains shortly what in his view, or the view of the Habad movement, is meant by accepting Judaism. It is "a pro-

---

[52] Landau, *Piety and Power - The World of Jewish Fundamentalism*: 298.
[53] Schochet, "Who is a Jew? 30 Questions and Answers About This Controversial and Divisive Issue". [05/12/2012].

found conviction of what the believer perceives as absolute truth regarding the ultimate values of life, or reality. Religion teaches the concepts of God, revelation, morality, ethical conduct, man's purpose, afterlife, and so forth, and it alone defines its perception and definition of these."[54] The future proselyte has to have a basic knowledge of Judaism. Further, the would-be convert has to have the conviction that Judaism reflects his perception of truth, and, finally, this future proselyte must be convinced that she/he has the desire and willingness to follow this truth in practice. If a conversion takes place which is not in accordance with all the above mentioned points the conversion was not conducted in a halakhic way and therefore the convert remains a gentile.[55]

If we agree with this statement, we could go a step further and explain why this happens. A gentile that converts under the auspices of, for instance, a Reform rabbi is afterwards, because of the missing halakhic procedure, still a gentile. If she/he converts under Orthodox auspices, the gentile becomes a Jew. This, though, only happens because, as a matter of fact, in the ideology of the Habad movement the respective convert never has been a real gentile. In her/him a holy spark has always resided. In the words of the Rebbe, "it is never the non-Jew who converts, for the one who converts does so because there is a holy spark within him, but for some reason it fell into a place to which it does not belong, and when he converts – after several prompts and attempts – then the holy spark is liberated and it joins the 'torch' and the 'light,' that is, the Torah, the commandments, and the blessed holy One."[56] If one follows the explanation of R. Schneerson, a convert, who finally becomes a Jew, was already endowed with a Jewish spark (holy spark) within her/him. The several attempts referred presumably to conversions, which happened at first under a Reform rabbi, or other non-Orthodox rabbis, but finally with a rabbi of the Habad movement.

It seems that it is just a religious discussion about the correct conversion to Judaism and its accompanying consequences. Schochet, however, is of the opinion that, with an improper conversion, the respective gentile thinks of her-/himself that she/he is a Jew and behaves accordingly. Though as a

---

[54] Ibid. [05/12/2012].

[55] Cf ibid. [05/12/2012].

[56] Citation taken from Wolfson, *Open Secret - Postmessianic Messianism and the Mystical Revision of Menahem Mendel Schneerson*: 261.

non-correct Jew, this may endanger the beginning of redemption. "This does not bring the Messiah closer, but rather repels and distances him."[57]

Furthermore, the 'Who is a Jew?' debate in Israel is of importance, as with the entry of non-Jews the danger of un-Jewish marriages rises, especially with an identity card of Israel that is in fact a political decision to let people immigrate, but with the wrong token these 'Jewish gentiles' do endanger the Jewish society on the whole. In the logic of R. Schochet with un-Orthodox conversions, which were not in the halakhic way, marriages are contracted in an improper way, as they are not Jewish anymore. It is, in consequence, according to this rabbi, a problem for all Jews, as the Jews represent one entity, "like unto one body with one heart and one soul, it is a tragedy affecting everyone."[58]

Arguments about political decisions by the State of Israel are illegitimate as the State of Israel could let other people immigrate as well, but not under the *Law of Return*. If one comes to Israel under the *Law of Return*, one receives an identity card that signifies that one is Jewish. In consequence, it complicates the situation for the persons who want to marry each other. It would lead to unwanted 'inter-marriages,' as R. Schochet calls the problem. "It is ... different, though, when they come from Israel armed with an Israeli passport and an Israeli identity-card which states that the bearer is 'Jewish.' This must, and will, lead to chaos and tragedy in terms of unwitting intermarriages, and/or the traumatic effects when discovering before or after a marriage that this Israeli groom or bride is in effect non-Jewish."[59] Therefore, the State of Israel, as a state which refers to itself as a Jewish state, has to add in its *Law of Return* that only orthodox conversions are seen as justified, as long as these conversions are supervised and guarded by a *dayan* in a *beit din* (court). Only then it is guaranteed that the Jewish society remains Jewish. Proselytes are only accepted, in the logic of the Habad movement, if they converted under special conditions, otherwise they remain gentiles. Nevertheless, the State of Israel with its representative body, the Knesset, is not the proper organ to discuss the topic of 'Who is a Jew?'. Though, the Knesset or any other political organs in Israel have

---

[57] Friedman, "Habad as Messianic Fundamentalism - From Local Particularism to Universal Jewish Mission," 351.

[58] Schochet, "Who is a Jew? 30 Questions and Answers About This Controversial and Divisive Issue". [05/13/2012].

[59] Ibid. [05/13/2012].

to guarantee that the Jewishness in the state remains intact. None of the cases which were tried in the Supreme Court fit this claim.

I discussed in detail the answer of R. Schochet on the question of 'Who is a Jew?', but it is still not clear how a Jew is meant to be. According to Yanki Tauber, an Israeli Habad author, Jews "defy all conventional definitions of a 'people' or 'nation.' We [Jews] lack a common race, culture or historical experience. While we [Jews] all share our eternal rights to the Land of Israel, for all but a few centuries of the last 4,000 years the overwhelming majority of Jews have not lived or even set foot in the Jewish homeland."[60] Tauber sees more the aspect of the chosenness by G-d as the primary reason of connection between all Jews. However, this connection between G-d and the Chosen ones is the Torah. "The substance of this relationship, the charter of this commitment, is the Torah. The Torah is G-d's concept of reality as communicated to man, the blueprint that describes the perfected world envisioned by its Creator and details the manner in which the Inventor of Life wishes it to be lived."[61] The Torah, which is the essential work in Judaism, is the connector between G-d and H-s people: "Through Torah, the Jew touches base with his own quintessential self and makes his intrinsic bond with his Creator a reality in his daily life."

In summation, a Jew is a person, according to the Habad theology, who is defined through the holy spark that resides in his soul. This spark makes his soul 'a part of G-d' H-mself. In view of the Kabbalistic maxim 'G-d, the Torah and Israel are one' – the Torah is a part of the bond of unity. This triple connection is what constitutes the Jewish people's character as 'the Chosen People.'[62] To ideally keep the Chosen clean of gentiles, conversions

---

[60] Yanki Tauber, "What Makes a Jew 'Jewish'?," Chabad.org, http://www.chabad.org/-library/article_cdo/aid/45132/jewish/What-Makes-a-Jew-Jewish.htm. [05/13/2012].

[61] Ibid. [05/13/2012].

[62] R. Schneur Zalman of Lyady writes in Tanya a very important chapter about the unity of all Jewish souls: "The root of every *nefesh, ruach* and *neshamah* [every soul in a Jew consists of these three parts], from the highest [soul] of all ranks to the lowest [soul] that is embodied within the illiterate and the most worthless, all derive, as it were, from the Supreme Mind which is *Chochmah Ilaah* (Supernal Wisdom). ... [T]hey remain bound and united with a wonderful and essential unity with their original essence and entity; namely, the extension of *Chochmah Ilaah* (Supernal Wisdom), inasmuch as the nurture and life of the *nefesh, ruach* and *neshamah* of the ignorant are drawn from the *nefesh, ruach* and *neshamah* of the saints and sages, the heads of Israel in their generation. [Emphasis in original.]" R. Schneur Zalman of Lyady, "Tanya -

have to be in an Orthodox manner and guided and supervised by a *dayan*, because non-Jews, who converted wrongly, 'in the clothes of Jews' may hurt the whole Jewish society. The danger may be "death, madness, or heresy, probably of an antinomian variety,"[63] if one does not convert correctly in halakhic way. A Jew ultimately has to be able to make spiritual journeys.

This has to happen to shorten the time until the beginning of redemption or bring redemption closer to the actual existence of humanity. However, this is not supposed to be misunderstood. The Habadniks accept every Jew[64] as far as she/he is halakhically a Jew. The Habad movement does only see the problems of invalid conversions. Even people remaining gentiles in regard of the Habad movement do not matter. The Habadniks are only concerned about the conversion procedure.

The State of Israel is responsible for the *Law of Return*, as the State of Israel claims to be a Jewish state. On the one hand, the Knesset is a political organ and not religious at all, but as it is able to formulate laws, it has to guarantee a Jewish life within Israel's borders. Otherwise, it cannot claim to be a Jewish state. Though on the other hand, the State of Israel, represented through the Knesset, is not responsible for the whole discussion about the question 'Who is a Jew?,' but only the religious representatives, the Chief Rabbinate, are responsible for this matter. They are, however, only able to validate the conversions as far as they enjoy the ability to do this, but the Chief Rabbinate cannot formulate laws since they have to be passed by the Knesset. This is the reason why the Habad movement got actively involved

---

Likutei Amarim, Chapter 2," Kehot Publication Society, http://www.chabad.org/library/tanya/tanya_cdo/aid/1028875/jewish/Chapter-2.htm. [05/23/2012].

[63] Loewenthal, *Communicating the Infinite - The Emergence of Habad School*: 12.

[64] This is corroborated by Mindel, *The Divine Commandments*: 43. Mindel explains in a few words the Habad ideology: "This ... should be said, that the warm attitude toward the simple, honest Jew, is one of the fundamental principles of Chabad. Paradoxical though it may seem – for Chabad, meaning *Wisdom, Understanding, Knowledge*, is a highly intellectual study – the idea that *all* Jews have a soul which is a 'part of the Divine above,' and consequently, even the unlearned Jew has inherent qualities on a par with those of the scholar, runs like a golden thread throughout the Chabad literature. [Emphasis in original.]" Further, there is, as substantiation, to cite from the letter which was written by the Rebbe to Ben-Gurion in 1959. The Rebbe "categorically rejected the idea of a 'secular Jew,' since Jewish identity is intricately linked to the pneumatic connection of the Jew, regardless of his or her allegiance, to the divine essence." Wolfson, *Open Secret - Postmessianic Messianism and the Mystical Revision of Menahem Mendel Schneerson*: 233.

in Israeli politics, as the movement wanted that the Halakhah version of conversion is amended to the *Law of Return*. The Habad movement knows itself that they enjoy only limited influence.

2. Six Day War

This war in June 1967 changed the situation for the State of Israel forever; notwithstanding the capturing of the West Bank, the Gaza Strip and the eastern part of Jerusalem, including the Temple Mount with the Western Wall, the Golan Heights also came into Israel's possession.

I describe the situation of the Six Day War in a few words including its prelude and aftermath, after this I take a look at the reaction or action of the Habad movement.

The Six Day War was mainly based on error and mutual miscalculation, because the Soviet Regime informed Egypt about a possible Israeli attack on Syria. The Soviet intelligence confirmed Egyptian officials of vague Syrian reports of Israeli troop arrangements on the border to Syria. Notwithstanding Israel's saber-rattling, there was no intention to deploy more forces on Syria's borders and a war with Syria was out of question for Israel at the time.

In contrast, for Israel war was a question of a 'Second Holocaust' – thus the newspaper *Haaretz*, for instance, published the Egyptian president Gamal Abdel Nasser's declaration of May 26: "If Israel wants war – well then, Israel will be destroyed!" and compared it with Hitler's statement of January 30, 1939: "If the Jews drag the world into war – world Jewry will be destroyed."[65] Israelis thought that they had to defend their lives, their families, and their homes.

The Six Day War, thus, had to start with a surprising attack on the Egyptian Air Force in Sinai. Almost everything of it was destroyed by the Israeli Air Force (IAF). Ezer Weizman of the IDF executive phoned his wife in the morning of day one and told her: "We have won the war."[66] The on-going air attacks of the IAF demoralized all Arab armies and finally forced them to collapse. Not only did the IAF offer great work, the IDF also entered the Sinai Peninsula after the IAF's first strike. Out of confusion in the Egyptian forces, Israeli soldiers easily wiped them off the Peninsula, which was accomplished by June 8th.

---

[65] Both citations taken from Benny Morris, *Righteous Victims - A History of the Zionist-Arab Conflict, 1881 - 2001* (New York: Vintage Books, 2001). 308.

[66] Citation taken from ibid., 318.

On June 6th, now also in a state of war with Jordan, Prime Minister Levi Eshkol gave permission to enter the Old City. In the shade of a soon coming truce with Jordan, ordered by the UN Security Council, the IDF had to work fast, and finished their operations until June 8th.

Syria was involved in the war, but was not seriously taken care of until June 9th. The reason to conquer the Golan Heights is based on former years' harassment by the Syrian army. The attack on June 9th was successful, not only because of an advantage in the air-force (as the Syrian air force was also destroyed, as the Egyptian and Jordanian ones), but relied on the fact that Syrians knew that the other armies were uplifted – in the end, the Golan Heights were conquered by the IDF.

The war was over after only six days of consecutive fighting. The victory of Israel over the armies of Egypt, Jordan, and Syria was out of the question. Further, Israel occupied land of every country, the Sinai Peninsula, the Gaza Strip, the West Bank, and the Golan Heights. It was some kind of miracle not only for religious people in Israel, but also for the *Hilonim*, who were astounded by the result of this war. *Haaretz* published: "The glory of past ages no longer is to be seen at a distance but is, from now on, part of the new state, and its illumination will irradiate the constructive enterprise of a Jewish society that is a link in the long chain of the history of the people in its country ... Jerusalem is all ours. Rejoice and celebrate, O dweller in Zion!"[67]

The aftermath of the war started with heated debates about the freshly taken areas – to hold this *land for peace*, for example,[68] was declined by Egypt and Jordan. Menachem Begin and some persons of the National Religious Party demanded annexation of all of the West Bank and the Gaza Strip – to keep it as historic parts of the 'Land of Israel.' At least they succeeded with the annexation of East Jerusalem and the surrounding part of Jerusalem on June 25-27. In these days of 1967 the areas were declared to be a part of Jerusalem's expanded municipal area. One can derive from the annexation of Jerusalem that the West Bank was not of such a high interest for the Israeli government. This is corroborated with a release: "United Jerusalem will remain within the territory of the State of Israel (special arrangements will be made for the sites that are sacred to the various relig-

---

[67] Citation taken from ibid., 329.

[68] See The Land for Peace Principle in Rabinovich and Reinharz, *Israel in the Middle East - Documents and Readings on Society, Politics, and Foreign Relations, Pre-1948 to the Present*, 238-39.

ions); as an interim stage, a military situation will remain in the West Bank; an effort will be made to seek a constructive solution for the long term; [a] self-government (autonomy) [will there be] for the local inhabitants."[69]

In September of 1967 the *Land of Israel Movement* (*LIM*) was founded. It consisted of seventy-two prominent persons who claimed that the borders must be retained by Israel. Notwithstanding *LIM*, religious nationalists, who rallied around the famous Rabbi Avraham Yitzhak Hacohen Kook, cried out that the miraculous conquests are the start of the divine redemption – *at'halta dege'ula*. Therefore, it is absolutely consequent, according to their argumentation, to annex and settle in the territories – it is a divine commandment. The next year Gush Emunim was founded, which wanted to map a 'Greater Israel' – *Eretz Israel Hashlema*.[70] Gush Emunim will be extensively discussed in the next chapter.

The national-religious Jews saw it without further consideration as a sign of G-d to give Israel the land, which belongs to Jews. The Habadniks also left a similar impression, as *the Rebbe* Schneerson took a hawkish position after the war and demanded that not one inch must be returned to the Arab states.[71] Other Haredim were as well convinced that the Six-Day War victory was a G-dly signature.[72]

The Habad Rebbe had had a foreshadowing of an upcoming war. One may assume that *the Rebbe* was able to see the future, according to the *Merkavah mystic*[73] it is possible that one has "the ability to know the future, to know the secret sins of every individual as well as the problematic aspects of his genealogy, and to be able, with theurgic power, to withstand attack by any enemy."[74] Already in the prelude of war *the Lubavitcher Rebbe* told his Habadniks that they should not be afraid. They should be, in contrast, confident and encouraged. As *the Rebbe* gave his speech on *Lag B'Omer* (in 1967 it was May 28), he knew of threats of the Egyptian army and a plethora of more pieces of information, but he was convinced of his thoughts: "Jews in the Land of Israel should remain there in confidence, for God had prom-

---

[69] Citation taken from Akiva Eldar and Idith Zertal, *Lords of the Land - The War Over Israel's Settlements in the Occupied Territories, 1967 - 2007* (New York: Nation Books, 2007). 6-7.

[70] Cf Morris, *Righteous Victims - A History of the Zionist-Arab Conflict, 1881 - 2001*: 302-46.

[71] Cf Landau, *Piety and Power - The World of Jewish Fundamentalism*: XIX.

[72] Cf Milton Viorst, *What Shall I Do with this People? - Jews and the Fractious Politics of Judaism* (New York, London: The Free Press, 2002). 8.

[73] This is a *kabbalistic* kind of mysticism, not unusually in the Habad movement.

[74] Loewenthal, *Communicating the Infinite - The Emergence of Habad School*: 8-9.

ised that [Lev. 26:6] 'I shall bring peace to the land.'"[75] A few days later, on Shabbat, he reassured the worried people: "In the current situation, we must pay great care to see to it that every Jew will put on tefillin [phylacteries], for this is a mitzvah that has great power to bring the Jews out from their difficulties in peace."[76] Furthermore, he did rely on the Talmud (*Babylonian Talmud* (B.T.), *Menachot 44a*) that for all of them, who don phylacteries, a long life will be granted. He quoted the Talmudic interpretation (B.T., *Brachot 6a*) of the verse that "all nations will fear you" and put it into relation with the *tefillin* on the head. In *the Rebbe's* conclusion, everyone who looks at Jews with their *tefillin* is overthrown with the fear of heaven, *yiras shomayim*. "Every Jew who would don tefillin on behalf of those who are in the army [presumably a reference to Israeli soldiers] would thereby help them so that they would live long and the fear of them would fall upon all those who surrounded them."[77]

As described, Israel won the war with tremendous territorial gain, including the Old City with the Western Wall; hence, *the Rebbe* himself claimed the victory and explained that soldiers by donning *tefillin* or persons, who donned *tefillin* for the IDF, were eventually responsible for the victory, as they frightened the enemies. In the conclusion of the Habadniks and *the Rebbe*, Israel had not been existent because of the Zionists, but was now existent because of *the Rebbe's* campaign.[78] In contrast to the aforementioned national-religious Jews, who saw the time of redemption drawing closer after the victorious war, *the Rebbe* saw it differently and perceived the significance of the war before it even happened.

Israel was left alone, a second Shoa could have happened, but it did not happen. *The Rebbe* saw in this abandonment a clear sign of G-d, because only G-d helped to avoid Israel's destruction; not only this, but also to be victorious. In this pattern *the Rebbe* linked the rescue of Israel's People in the Exodus from Egypt in biblical times to victory.[79] This was not enough for *the Rebbe*. As the charismatic leader of the Habad movement he for sure represented the opinion of almost all Habadniks in the world, and thus he

---

[75] Citation taken from Samuel C. Heilman and Menachem Friedman, *The Rebbe - The Life and Afterlife of Menachem Mendel Schneerson* (Princeton, NJ [u.a.]: Princeton Univ. Press, 2010). 187.

[76] Citation taken from ibid.

[77] Citation taken from ibid.

[78] Cf ibid., 187-88.

[79] Cf ibid., 201-02.

went on that the war was not won because of military superiority, but that Israel's soldiers won, because they acted as Jews by donning *tefillin* and not as *goyim* (non-Jews). The Habad movement sees the Jews as a unique people, which according to them is the Chosen People.[80] This runs counter to the loathing of Jews by antisemites, but *the Rebbe* connects it, as he is well-versed, with Numbers 23:9: "Lo, the people shall dwell alone." One has to know, if one is a Jew, that she/he is connected to the 'everlasting Torah.' The Holy Book 'alone will protect us,'[81] as I indicated in the last argument.

We reach the question, what the intention of *the Rebbe* to put so much effort in the Six Day War was? The authors of an excellent biography of *the Rebbe* Menachem Mendel Schneerson, Samuel Heilman and Menachem Friedman, see Messianism in the Six Day War and its aftermath in the Lubavitcher Hasidic movement. But Edward Hoffman, who wrote a book about the Lubavitcher movement as well, has an absolute different point of view, which he proofed with declarations by *the Rebbe*. *The Rebbe* based all his considerations about the war and the on-going status of the occupied territories on Jewish law. *The Rebbe* Schneerson saw a danger to the lives of Jews and the saving of them (*pikuach nefesh*) supersedes every other scenario one could have in mind.[82]

Both authors may be right. Above I briefly discussed the theology of the Habad movement, thus it is possible to use both arguments as a base. Hoffman claims that he used a declaration of *the Rebbe* himself, which can be proved as the declaration is seen in several videos.[83] Hence, I first discuss Hoffman's claim; afterwards I take a look at the Messianistic assertion of Heilman/Friedman.

But foremost, we take into consideration that *the Rebbe* wanted that every Habadnik, better every male Jew, even better if he is a soldier, shall pray with *tefillin* in time of war. The reason for donning *tefillin* is, as claimed by

---

[80] This is also supported by Mindel, *The Divine Commandments*: 28. As Mindel states: "'[The Torah] is a tree of life to those that take fast hold of it' (Proverbs 3:18) ... Herein lies the secret of the eternity of the Jew, the secret of his survival, the strength of his spirit. That is why, so long as the Jew will cling to his Torah and faith, there is no power on earth that can destroy the Jewish people."

[81] Cf Heilman and Friedman, *The Rebbe - The Life and Afterlife of Menachem Mendel Schneerson*: 202.

[82] Cf Hoffman, *Despite All Odds - The Story of Lubavitch*: 162-63.

[83] See e.g. unknown, "The Six Day War and Teffilin," Jewish Educational Media, http://www.chabad.org/multimedia/media_cdo/aid/397220/jewish/The-Six-Day-War-and-Tefillin.htm. [03/19/2012].

Schneerson, that a Jew falls into a different category, as a tractate in Talmud about *Rosh Hashanah* affirms.[84] Notwithstanding the donned phylacteries by Jews, who can connect with each G-dly soul,[85] *the Rebbe* also quoted Zechariah (4:6): "Neither by might, nor by power, but by my spirit, saith the Lord of hosts."[86] All in all on gets the impression that, according to *the Rebbe's* thinking, G-d H-mself won the Six Day War. The connection with the G-dly soul, *nefesh elokhit*, and *Tefillin* leads directly to *Ayin*. As I explained in the part about the theology of the Habad movement, *Ayin* is usually seen as G-d and thus has to be connected with *nefesh elokhit*. Therefore, a connection *en masse* of *nefeshim elokhitot* leads to a stronger bond with G-d. As there is nothing besides H-m, G-d is also *Yesh*, the world. There is a more stringent bond with H-m and the world, or *Yesh*. Jews with *Tefillin* and their active *nefesh elokhit* set the animal soul, *nefesh bahamit*, out of work. In other words, the Jew has to negate himself to come into connection with G-d. This is called *bitul* (selfabnegation). Through prayer with phylacteries the soldier of the IDF, for instance, is able to ascend his G-dly soul and to restore the divine unity. The soldier is reduced to "nought but the Divine flowing through him. Yet he is still a man in human world."[87] It leaves a good start for the connection of the naught with reality. "Just as they [i.e. the worlds of *Yesh* and *Ayin*] are united by His power [G-d's power], may He be blessed, in the aspect of upper unification (yihuda 'ila'a), so must they be united in the aspect of the lower unification (yihuda tata'a), that they [human beings] be annihilated towards Him, may He be blessed, that they not be made manifest as existing and separate in terms of their own essence."[88] This means that the soldier prays, while he does this, he forces his *nefesh elokhit* to ascend, thus his soul leaves any corporeality. *Nefesh elokhit* unites itself with G-d, when this is done the divine unity is

---

[84] Cf Benzion Rader, "Why Teffilin?," Chabad.org, http://www.chabad.org/therebbe/article_cdo/aid/133500/jewish/Why-Tefillin.htm. [03/19/2012].

[85] Cf Rebbe Nachman of Breslev, "Teffilin - the Skin of Imagination," Chabad.org, http://www.chabad.org/kabbalah/article_cdo/aid/380355/jewish/Tefillin-Skin-of-the-Imagination.htm. [03/19/2012].

[86] Citation taken of Heilman and Friedman, *The Rebbe - The Life and Afterlife of Menachem Mendel Schneerson*: 202.

[87] Loewenthal, *Communicating the Infinite - The Emergence of Habad School*: 32.

[88] Citation taken from Rachel Elior, "HaBaD - The Contemplative Ascent to God," in *Jewish Spirituality - From the Sixteenth Century Revival to the Present*, ed. Arthur Green, *World Spirituality - An Encyclopedic History of the Religious Quest* (London: Routledge & Kegan Paul, 1987), 179. in: Sha'arey ha-Yihud weha-Emunah, V:19.

restored. This takes place in *Ayin*, but as there is nothing besides H-m, it has to take place at the same time in *Yesh* as well. Then the soldier's soul is *nefesh elokhit* suppressing *nefesh bahamit*, with this the soldier has a connection to G-d. This gives him an awareness, which frightens his foes, at least in the logic of *the Rebbe*.

Notwithstanding, *nefesh elokhit* is also seen in Habad theology as one pole, which is the Infinite (*Ein Sof*), the holiness, unity, revelation, and the Good Urge.[89] This 'pole' has to be brought about by prayer, at best with phylacteries, on earth – to 'force' G-d's help down to earth, to *Yesh*; which is connected with the formerly discussed argument. This was already mentioned by R. Aaron Ha-Levi (b. 1235 (?) – d. 1300), a *Kabbalist* of the Middle Ages: "The essential worship is to draw down the light of the Infinite, blessed be He, into the realm of the Finite, that the glory of God be revealed specifically in the sense of manifestation of the Finite, and in this worship ... the essential intention is revealed in its inwardness."[90] Even if this contradicts the above discussed argument, we have to keep in mind that the theology of the Habad movement is paradox and that the world is an illusion[91] to human mind, notwithstanding that human mind is not able to understand this, and one has to take it as a Habadic fact that there is nothing besides H-m.[92]

After the Six Day War with the incredible land gains, the Habad movement, with *the Rebbe* as its leader, claimed the success; *tefillin* prayer was mainly responsible for it, in other words – G-d H-mself. What should be done with the land gains? As mentioned, Heilman/Friedman and Hoffman contradict each other. The former, on the one hand, claim a kind of Messianism and Hoffman, on the other hand, cites a speech of *the Rebbe* in which

---

[89] Cf ibid., 176.

[90] Citation taken from ibid., 179. in: Sha'arey ha-Avodah, I:33.

[91] "Even though it appears to us that the worlds exist, this is a total lie." Citation taken from ibid., 161. in: R. Shneur Zalman, Torah Or, Tisa, p.86b.

[92] This claim is proved through a look in *Tanya*, the work of the first Rebbe. In the middle of chapter 37 of the book *Likutei Amarim* of the *Tanya* complex is written: "G-d is the L-rd; there is nothing else besides H-m." R. Schneur Zalman of Lyady, "Likutei Amarim Chapter 37," Kehut Publication Society, http://www.chabad.org/-library/tanya/tanya_cdo/aid/7916/jewish/Chapter-37.htm. [03/21/2012]. Further, chapter 33 speaks about the aloneness of G-d: "He is One alone in the upper and lower realms, just as He was alone prior to the six days of Creation. Even in the very place where the world – the heaven, the earth and all their host – was created, He alone then filled this space. The same is true now: He is One alone, without any change whatever." of Lyady, "Likutei Amarim Chapter 33". [03/21/2012].

he said that it is a danger of the Jew in question, no inch, therefore, is to be returned. In so far Heilman/Friedman both agree with Hoffman; they disagree only on the demand of *the Rebbe* to withhold the newly taken territories.

Hoffman's thesis is to be proven with Habad theology. Jews are in danger – therefore *pikuach nefesh* is demanded, thus the respective souls should be saved. This is corroborated by Yanki Tauber. He agrees with *the Rebbe* about the future of the conquered land. Tauber, in accordance with *the Rebbe*, claims that no land has to be given up. Tauber elaborates this point further relying on the *Shulchan Aruch*, section 329 of the Code's first book *Orach Hayim*.

"The law describes the following scenario: A hostile army attacks you, or threatens to attack you, and demands a piece of territory. They say, 'Give us this piece of land, and we'll leave you alone.' The overriding issue is pikuach nefesh, saving lives, which supersedes the entire Torah. Do we go to war to prevent the enemy's occupation of the territory, or do we relinquish the territory in return for a promise of future non-aggression?"[93]

The commentary of the *Alter Rebbe*, R. Schneur Zalman of Lyady, concludes from the law in section 329, as follows: "Anything necessary must be done if there is a possibility that it will save or prolong someone's life."[94] In other words, it is presumably ambiguous, notwithstanding one has to save lives. This was taken into consideration when discussing the land gains after the Six Day War.[95]

All in all, the land had to remain in the hands of Israel to avoid the danger of being attacked by Egypt, Jordan, or Syria, even if Israel desired peace. The first idea of Israel's government was to give up *land for peace*, with the exception of the annexed territories around East Jerusalem and East Jerusalem herself. The giving up of any newly gained area or a partial responsibility, for instance, in the West Bank, as suggested by Yigal Allon,[96] cannot be good, as Yanki Tauber's remarks are based as well on *the Rebbe's* thinking. It is worthy to cite a paragraph of his blog:

---

[93] Yanki Tauber, "Land for Peace?," Chabad.org, http://www.chabad.org/library-/article_cdo/aid/82019/jewish/Land-for-Peace.htm. [05/15/2012].

[94] R. Schneur Zalman of Lyady, "Schulchan Aruch - Orach Chaim," 2000 Project Genesis, http://www.torah.org/advanced/shulchan-aruch/classes/orachchayim/chapter24.html. [03/21/2012].

[95] Cf Tauber, "Land for Peace?". [03/22/2012].

[96] Cf Morris, *Righteous Victims - A History of the Zionist-Arab Conflict, 1881 - 2001*: 330-31.

"That's why G-d gave us the Torah – a set of truths that are not the product of our brains, but of the inherent truths upon which He predicated His creation of reality and the universe. The Torah's purpose is not to absolve us of the need to use our brains – on the contrary, it expects us to work the brain to death comprehending the what, why and how of the truths it embodies. But it does enable us to know when our brain is running backwards. If the end result of our reasoning and logicizing doesn't mesh with the divine truths contained in the Torah, we're doing something wrong. The people of Israel desperately desire peace. And we desperately desire that our enemies should desire this as much as we do. We are simply not prepared to accept a reality that contradicts this all-consuming desire."[97]

The Rebbe sees the whole situation, probably from a different historic context, as follows:

"With regard to the liberated areas, military experts, Jewish and non-Jewish, agree that in the present situation, giving up any part of them would create serious dangers. No one says that relinquishing any part of them would enhance the defensibility of the borders. But some military experts are prepared to take a chance in order not to antagonize the American government and/or to improve Israel's 'international image.' To follow this line of reasoning would not only contradict the clear verdict, but also ignore costly lessons of the past."[98]

In the eyes of *the Rebbe* the Arab states were militarily prepared to attack Israel. In this aspect he was right, as Israel was surprised by the attack at Yom Kippur in 1973; therefore his reliance on the *Shulchan Aruch* was justified: "The Arab neighbors are prepared militarily. What is more, they demand these areas as theirs to keep and openly declare that if not surrendered by Israel voluntarily, they will take them by force and eventually everything else."[99]

One usually expects of a Jewish religious leader that he invokes the biblical meaning of the Holy Land. *The Rebbe*, in contrast, spoke about the newly taken territories and did not refer to the biblical reference of the areas. Indeed, he stated it is irrelevant what kind of biblical land it is – foremost *nefesh pikuach* is of higher importance; "it is the duty of every Jew – whether lay person or rabbi – to do all that is permitted by the Codes of

---

[97] Tauber, "Land for Peace?". [03/23/2012].

[98] Citation taken from Hoffman, *Despite All Odds - The Story of Lubavitch*: 163.

[99] Citation taken from ibid., 164.

Jewish Law [*Shulchan Aruch*] to help forestall or minimize the military danger to Israel. In a case of 'danger to life,' every possible effort must be made even if one doubts whether the effort will succeed."[100]

All this is supported by a part of the *Tanya*:

"Nevertheless, the Rabbis declared, 'Not learning, but doing is the essential thing.' It is also written, 'This day to do them.' And [it has been ruled that] one should interrupt the study of the Torah in order to fulfil [sic!] an active precept that cannot be performed by others. For, 'This is the whole man,' and the purpose of his creation and his descent to this world, in order that He have an abode here below especially, to turn darkness into light, so that the glory of the Lord shall fill all of this material world."[101]

In other words, Jews have to forget all their studies of Torah to save souls of other Jews in the same manner as their own. One has to keep in mind that neither R. Yosef Karo referred to the aftermath of the Six Day War nor that the *Alter Rebbe* did, but from my perspective, as the *Shulchan Aruch* and *Tanya* are taken still as valid by the Habad movement and *the Rebbe* himself, it is possible to substantiate the claims of *the Rebbe*, who alluded to the Jewish Law Code with the commentary of the *Alter Rebbe* and *Tanya*.

We can conclude that *the Rebbe* brought *nefesh pikuach* to the forefront. He was clearly convinced that any Jew is more worth than any Arab. He did not invoke on the biblical meaning of the newly occupied areas, but on the Jews' souls that had to be saved – as the whole case rallies around the Halakah and on nothing else; the conquest of biblical territories is only a positive side effect.

Hoffman's part about the aftermath of the Six Day War did not mention the issue of Messianism – in contrast to Heilman/Friedman. They paid more attention to Messianism according to *the Rebbe*, which was maybe implied in the reaction of *the Rebbe* to the land gains – notwithstanding *the Rebbe's* standpoint that Israel, even if a haven for many Jews and Judaism *per se*, has "nothing to do with the Redemption or the Beginnings of the Redemption."[102] In other words, Israel is not seen as anything else but a secular state on the globe. Every Jew, according to the theology of Habad,

---

[100] Citation taken from ibid., 164-65.

[101] R. Schneur Zalman of Lyady, "Tanya Likutei Amarim Chapter 37," Kehot Publication Society, http://www.chabad.org/library/tanya/tanya_cdo/aid/1029047/jewish/-Chapter-37.htm. [03/23/2012].

[102] Citation taken from Hoffman, *Despite All Odds - The Story of Lubavitch*: 165.

does still live in *galut* (exile). Thus there is no Messianic spot in the world – at least for now.[103] The analysis of Heilman/Friedman takes it for granted that the Habad movement is a Messianic movement, therefore they neglect the exceptions. The statement about the importance of *nefesh pikuach* and that *the Rebbe* did explicitly not see the victory of the Six Day war as a sign of redemption was not taken into consideration by the authors. Nevertheless, there was Messianism in *the Rebbe's* thinking. How does this Messianism proven by the author-duo fit into Habad ideology for Israel?

It is necessary to take a look into the Habad theology to locate Messianism. At first, one comes across the following statement: "Even a Jew who lives in Jerusalem today says in his prayers, 'Because of our sins we were exiled from our Land.' For even one who is physically in the Land of Israel, is still in galut."[104]

It is no secret; the opposite of *galut*, in the idea of the Habad movement, is redemption (*geulah*). In Hebrew, only an *Aleph* has to be added to the middle of the word *galut* and it becomes *geulah*. The meaning of *Aleph* is *Alufo Shel Olam* – the Ruler of the World. It is also the first letter of the Hebrew alphabet, which represents the beginning of everything in Habad theology (based on Kabbalism). This is taken to a higher level, as G-d existed before creation and as G-d was the source for creation. Furthermore, *the Rebbe* Menachem Mendel Schneerson assumes that *Aleph* is the source of every Hebrew letter – in the theology of Habad, hence, the world is based on the letters of the Hebrew alphabet, with them G-d created the world.

If *galut* becomes *geulah*, the world changes with it. As the Jews are in exile/*galut* they suffer in uncountable situations. In redemption there will be no suffering for Jews anymore.[105]

The belief in redemption is validated with Maimonides and a glimpse into the Talmud. The Jew is going to be asked, when she/he faces the Heavenly Court: "Did you yearn for the Salvation?" In the Midrash (*Yalkut Shimoni*, Psalm 736) is similarly mentioned: "If the Jewish people have no merit other than their yearning for Redemption – they are worthy of being redeemed for that alone!"

---

[103] Cf unknown, "The Basics," Moshiach Campaign, Chabad.org, http://www-.chabad.org/library/moshiach/article_cdo/aid/1157488/jewish/The-Basics.htm. [03/28/2012].

[104] Ibid. [03/28/2012].

[105] Cf Rebbe Menachem Mendel Schneerson, "Exile+1 = Redemption," http://www.-chabad.org/library/moshiach/article_cdo/aid/1192683/jewish/Exile-1-Redemption.htm. [03/28/2012].

The Rebbe Menachem Mendel Schneerson announced more than once that the era of redemption is close. One has to increase the acts of goodness and kindness in order to be worthy to greet the redeemer – the Messiah. *The Rebbe* mentioned that more than a few global phenomena have happened, which are clear indicators for the coming of the redemption in near future.[106] One may assume that it was not only the disruption of the Soviet Union, but also the Israeli victory in the Six Day War, which *the Rebbe* referred to as 'global phenomena.' "It convinced him [*the Rebbe*] that the currents of history were leading to the fulfillment of the promise that the Messiah would come in his generation."[107] Heilman/Friedman suggested not only that *the Rebbe* was convinced of the coming of redemption, as it cannot be negated. The author-duo went on to see a clear link to redemption (*geulah*) in the victory of the Six-Day War:

"The Rebbe perceived the footsteps of the Messiah in the combination of the abandonment before the war [by the foreign supporters of Israel] and what he saw as the God-given Lubavitcher-led victory of the nation of Israel.

If Menachem Mendel had harbored any doubts about his understanding of the unfolding of events and his power to direct them, the developments in Israel after 1967 helped wipe them away and increased his confidence in his and his late father-in-law's role in ushering in the age of redemption. This led him ... to make ever more grandiose and extravagant claims. History no longer was a mystery but became instead the revelation of a plan for salvation the Lubavitcher rebbes – presumably the primary prophetic leaders of the Jews – had been pushing. And if the end was near, then, just as Menachem Mendel has promised in his Basi L'Gani talk at his crowning, this generation and its leader would be the ones to bring the Messiah."[108]

Finally, the perspective of the Habad movement in regard to the State of Israel took on the flavor saving Jews in the risk of danger, as "nobody is more concerned with the fate of Jews – every Jew – than the Rebbe."[109] The

---

[106] Cf unknown, "Belief and Anticipation - The Basics," Moshiach Campaign, Chabad.org, http://www.chabad.org/library/moshiach/article_cdo/aid/1121885/-jewish/The-Basics.htm. [03/28/2012].

[107] Heilman and Friedman, *The Rebbe - The Life and Afterlife of Menachem Mendel Schneerson*: 197.

[108] Ibid., 203.

[109] Ibid., 201.

Six Day War, as it turned out in the end, would be won before it even started, because of the faith in intensive praying with *tefillin* by soldiers of the IDF or by Habadniks, or any other Jew. The Six Day War was won with tremendous land gains. The position of *the Rebbe* as representative of the Habad movement was that no inch would be returned to Arab states – *'Land for Peace,'* for instance, was no option for the Habad movement. In this matter Hoffman and Heilman/Friedman agreed that the Habad movement wanted to keep the areas won. They disagreed on the reasons for their keeping. Hoffman, an author close to the Habad movement, often cited *the Rebbe*. These citations were proven and solid and, after I have tried to disprove them, they still ring true. In other words, the intention to keep the taken land is based on the *Shulchan Aruch*, Book *Orech Chaim*, Section 329, with the reaffirmation by the *Alter Rebbe* in his commentary on this section: *nefesh pikuach* – save the souls of Jews, if they are in danger. The danger may have been to give up land for peace and you will be attacked sooner than later with the disadvantage of having no land that serves as a puffer zone. Heilman/Friedman, though, found Messianism in the aftermath of the Six Day War in the reaction of the Habad movement to keep the land. This is true as well – as *the Rebbe* often spoke about redemption being close and announced several global occurrences, which give hints at *geulah*.

In summation, the Habad movement's interests in the politics of Israel were, at the time of the Six Day War including the prelude and aftermath, to take care of Jewish souls. There may have been also some kind of Messianism, but this contradicts one statement of *the Rebbe*. Nonetheless it cannot be excluded.

Chapter III: The settlement policy of the Habad movement and a comparison between the Habad movement and Gush Emunim

1. Common Overview of the Settlement Policy

In this argument I cover the common settlement policy in the West Bank and also in the Gaza Strip and Sinai Peninsula.[1] Moreover, I present the actual situation of the West Bank in figures. Then, I show the ascendency of Gush Emunim (bloc of faithful) and its present condition including its ideology. I take a special look at the theology of their source of inspiration: who are R. Abraham Issac Kook (b. 1891 – d. 1982) and his son R. Zvi Yehuda Kook (b. 1891 – d. 1982). Finally, I try to compare all with the perspectives of the Habad movement in reference to settlements in the occupied territories, its approach to them, and its respective *raison d'être*.

"Jewish settlement in the West Bank began ... in Jerusalem and its environs during the first days after the guns [of the Six Day War] fell silent."[2] The Jewish Quarter in the Old City, as was quickly decided, had to be resettled by Jews. The Arab population, which resided in it, fled without complaints.

As I mentioned in the argument about the 1967 war, the *LIM* in September 1967 and shortly afterwards a movement around R. Kook Jr., who was in charge of the yeshiva *Merkaz HaRav* in Jerusalem, was founded. His movement was loaded with messianic intentions. Thus, for instance, after the Old City had been taken by the IDF, a few disciples of R. Kook entered it heading to the Western Wall and proclaimed: "We hereby inform the people of Israel and the entire world that under heavenly command we have just returned home. ... We shall never move out."[3] It consequently led to the foundation of Gush Emunim.

Foremost I explain common settlement policy; at first, former Jewish occupations like the Etzion Bloc[4] or areas with a low density of Arabian resi-

---

[1] I do not take credit of the Golan Heights, as they were annexed by Law in 1981. The Heights are only under discussion between Syria and Israel, but they are not demanded by Palestinians.

[2] Morris, *Righteous Victims - A History of the Zionist-Arab Conflict, 1881 - 2001*: 331.

[3] Citation taken from ibid., 332.

[4] "We were prepared for the possibility of settling at Kfar Etzion without authorization, with the backing of the Greater Land of Israel movement people and others. ... We organized everything we needed on a truck that was parked at Moshav Nehalim. ...

dents were resettled. From then, on all regions were taken into consideration for settlements. The case of Kiryat Arba has to be highlighted, as in its
prelude a hotel was squatted by R. Moshe Levinger with R. Haim Druckman, Israel Harel, Benny Katzover, and R. Eliezer Waldman (all 'members'
of Gush Emunim in its wake), who only got the permission to stay for one
night in the hotel to hold a traditional *Pesach Seder*; they, however, refused
to leave the hotel the next morning.[5] They saw it as a Jewish right to settle
in Hebron, as it may have been "the burial place of the patriarchs and ma-
triachs of the Jewish nation."[6] After long negotiations it was concluded that
they were given the right to settle in what was later to become Kiryat Arba
close to Hebron.[7]

Building settlements was either state-organized or illegal. Construction
took place on former Jordanian territory or was directly purchased from
local landowners by state authorities or settler associations. "Frequently
Arab-owned lands were expropriated on ostensible security grounds but
were earmarked for settlement."[8] The settlers were of different social back-
grounds – "quite separately hundreds, and then thousands, of Jews, driven
by ideological motives ('Greater Israel') and economic incentives (free or
cheap land, big mortgages at low interest, outright grants), began to move
to the [conquered] territories."[9] Even though Gush Emunim and the *Land of
Israel Movement* hoped for people to move into the West Bank, interest
among them was low. Kiryat Arba, which became the first figurehead of
Gush Emunim, remained empty. Of 877 apartments over 450 were not ten-
anted, many families moved to other places. Kiryat Arba became a town in
which life was only hard and bitter, it was a small and shabby development town.[10]

Eshkol [the prime minister] asked us when wanted to move there and we replied to
pray there on Rosh Hashanah (October 5-6). Eshkol replied: 'Go ahead.'" This was
stated by Hannan Porat, one of the first settlers, who lived before 1948 in Kfar Etzion.
Citation taken from Eldar and Zertal, *Lords of the Land - The War Over Israel's
Settlements in the Occupied Territories, 1967 - 2007*: 11-12.

[5] Cf Morris, *Righteous Victims - A History of the Zionist-Arab Conflict, 1881 - 2001*: 334.

[6] Eldar and Zertal, *Lords of the Land - The War Over Israel's Settlements in the Occupied
Territories, 1967 - 2007*: 18.

[7] Cf Morris, *Righteous Victims - A History of the Zionist-Arab Conflict, 1881 - 2001*: 334-35.

[8] Ibid., 335.

[9] Ibid.

[10] Cf Eldar and Zertal, *Lords of the Land - The War Over Israel's Settlements in the Occupied
Territories, 1967 - 2007*: 28.

In figures, until 1977, when Menachem Begin took over the government, thirty-six settlements were built in the West Bank,[11] with a population up to 7,400 people. From 1978 onwards, when Begin was Prime Minister, the settlements almost doubled within six years from 39 (in 1978) to 76 (in 1983). The population in it tripled from circa 7,400 to 22,800 people. In the first year of Yitzhak Shamir as Prime Minister (1984) the settlements rose to 102 official settlements. The population reached the level of 35,300 residents.[12] In the up-coming years the legal settlements rose to 123 in 1998, with a population of 164,800 people. In 2005 the settlements were diminished to a total of 121 with a population growth totaling 247,514 residents. The statistics stops in 2009: 121 settlements with a population of 301,200 people in the West Bank.[13] In accordance with the international law the West Bank has the status of being occupied, but not annexed.

I continue with the different withdrawals of the State of Israel and the destruction of the settlements in the respective areas. The peace agreement

---

[11] Cf Morris, *Righteous Victims - A History of the Zionist-Arab Conflict, 1881 - 2001*: 335.

[12] The numbers of settlements and residents could only rise at such a spanking pace due to the help of Ariel Sharon, who did all to foster the life conditions of settlers. Further, the government annulled the prohibition for Jews to purchase Arab-owned land in the West Bank. Cf Eldar and Zertal, *Lords of the Land - The War Over Israel's Settlements in the Occupied Territories, 1967 - 2007*: 99.

[13] This refers to the West Bank with the exclusion of East Jerusalem. The data for East Jerusalem were recorded by *B'tselem* between 1989 and 2007. In this time the Jewish population rose from 118,100 to 184,707 people. Cf Eyal Hareuveni, *By Hook and by Crook - Israeli Settlement Policy in the West Bank*, ed. Yael Stein, trans. Zvi Shulman (B'tselem.org: B'tselem, 2010). 9-10. East Jerusalem is a delicate topic. On the one hand Jerusalem is united and East Jerusalem is annexed, though on the other hand mainly Arabs reside in East Jerusalem. Jerusalem's mayor Nir Barkat announced in April 2012 that 200 new houses in a disputed area between two Palestinian towns would be created and as well that they would be close to the supposedly new Palestinian parliament building. Cf Akiva Eldar and Nir Hasson, "Jerusalem Mayor aims to establish new settlement in East Jerusalem," Haaretz, http://www.haaretz.com/news/national/jerusalem-mayor-aims-to-establish-new-settlement-in-east-jerusalem-1.422228. [05/24/2012]. Because of the fact that for Israeli leaders Jerusalem is the capital city of Israel (including East Jerusalem), one does not have to wonder about the announcements of Prime Minister Netanyahu in which he demanded a continuation of the development in East Jerusalem; though without the intention to punish Palestinians. Cf Jonathan Lis and Natasha Mozgovaya, "Netanyahu: It is Israel's right and obligation to build in Jerusalem," Haaretz, http://www.haaretz.com/news/diplomacy-defense/netanyahu-it-is-israel-s-right-and-obligation-to-build-in-jerusalem-1.393341. [05/25/2012].

with Egypt in 1979 included the withdrawal from the Sinai Peninsula. The disengagement (*hitnatkut*) of the Sinai Peninsula was enforced in two stages. The first stage ran unhindered. The second one was overshadowed by the assassination of Anwar al-Sadat by the *Jihad Organization* (a sub-organization of the *Muslim Brotherhood*) and the discussions about the future of the Taba region in the Sinai Peninsula, but the argument was settled with the help of the Reagan administration.

"There remained the problem of Begin's domestic opponents, who since the summer of 1981 had mounted a campaign of harassment and demonstrations. From July 1981 onward Gush Emunim members and [other radical] West Bank settlers began moving illegally into empty apartments in Yamit, the main Jewish settlement in northeastern Sinai, and into other sites in the Rafa Approaches."[14] The 1,500 settlers[15] had to be 'liberated' by about 20,000 IDF soldiers. Yamit and all other settlements were erased by bulldozers to avoid offering the Egyptians readymade bases in the case of Cairo deciding to violate the peace treaty.[16] After the erasure, the long period of settling the Sinai Peninsula was over.

In 2005 the Gaza Strip evacuation took place, by order of Ariel Sharon, the then Prime Minister. The disengagement of the Strip began on August 17th and was accomplished five days later.

"The evacuation process ... consisted of the evacuation of approximately 8000 civilians, from 21 Israeli communities ... During the evacuation of the community of Kfar Darom, on August 18, 2005, approximately 200 civilians, mostly youths, barricaded themselves in the synagogue of the community. After dialogue ... failed, it was decided to ... remove those barricading themselves inside. ... At the same time, the IDF continues to remove the military infrastructure that served the Israeli security forces in the Gaza Strip. ... The completion of the evacuation of the Israeli residents and com-

---

14 Morris, *Righteous Victims - A History of the Zionist-Arab Conflict, 1881 - 2001*: 490-91.

15 These settlers were so-called *professional settlers* of the West Bank, who took the places of the original residents of Yamit. One of the former residents said to *Haaretz*: "I have a feeling that some of the elements operating in the area are clearly intending to foment a civil war! Such a war could serve their interests [of the settlers in the West Bank]. ... A national trauma of a civil war in the Yamit Region could serve as a warning to any government that would sit down in the future to discuss any agreements whatsoever about evacuating settlements in Judea and Samaria [as the West Bank is called]." Citation taken from Eldar and Zertal, *Lords of the Land - The War Over Israel's Settlements in the Occupied Territories, 1967 - 2007*: 72.

16 Cf Morris, *Righteous Victims - A History of the Zionist-Arab Conflict, 1881 - 2001*: 491.

munities of Gush Katif, Netzarim and the northern Gaza Strip, brings to a close an important chapter of 30 years of settlement."[17]

The withdrawal of the settlers from the Gaza Strip, however, was not as easy as stated by the IDF Spokesperson. The proclamation to implement the disengagement of the Gaza Strip was accompanied with demonstrations by whole communities, including women, children, and babies. Furthermore, political lobbies ventured to stop the plan before August 2005. Relativization of the Shoa was undertaken as well: "The evacuation of even one single settler [was compared with] the persecution of the Jews during the Holocaust period."[18] Sharon was described as a Nazi and his employees declared to be a *Judenrat* and *Kapos*. Yaakov Katz, a settlement leader, even called upon G-d for the sake of the demonstrations: "In this war against the Holy One, blessed be He, about the return to Zion, no one will prevail. Not even Arik Sharon."[19] Even though the actual disengagement of the Gaza Strip took place more than a year after the well-known rabbi R. Avigdor Neventzal had "said ... that anyone who gives away parts of the land of Israel to gentiles [in fact, the Gaza Strip to the responsibility of Palestinians] is open to a *din rodef* - a religious license to *kill a fellow Jew* [Emphasis added.]" – a whiff of assassination. Moreover, other settler leaders appealed to the respective soldiers for a disobedience to "their commanders' orders during the disengagement."[20] Nonetheless, the evacuation of the Gaza Strip went on and "the settlements were destroyed in an ungenerous move by an unenlightened occupier [the Israeli government], which in fact continues to control the territory and kill and harass its inhabitants by means of its formidable military might. ... The tragedy [of the disengagement] remains the exclusive province of the evacuated settlers themselves, not the Israelis as a whole."[21]

I return to the West Bank and its current situation; today the whole process of the settlement policy rallies around international pressure to demolish settlements, or moratoria in settlement building.

---

[17] IDF-Spokesman, "Evacuation of Israeli civilians from the Gaza Strip completed," Ministry of Foreign Affairs, http://www.mfa.gov.il/MFA/Government/Communiques/2005/Evacuation+of+Israeli+civilians+from+the+Gaza+Strip+completed+2-2-Aug-2005.htm. [05/23/2012].

[18] Eldar and Zertal, *Lords of the Land - The War Over Israel's Settlements in the Occupied Territories, 1967 - 2007*: 448.

[19] Citation taken from ibid.

[20] Ibid.

[21] Ibid., 450.

I highlight a discussion about single houses, which were built on Palestinian ground or had already been bought by the World Zionist Organization.[22] According to *Israelnetz.com*, in 2011 the Supreme Court declared that all buildings illegally built on private Palestinian land have to be demolished.[23] A *Haaretz* commentary shows that this uprooting of a few houses may be compared to the 'legal' uprooting of the settlements in the Gaza Strip. According to the Supreme Court it was legal to demolish the households; it had, however, before Sharon had been legal the idea to evacuate the Gaza Strip to live there.[24] It is a hotly disputed discussion and the opinions seesaw between an agreement to uproot houses and keep them, because of the sake of Israeli settlers.[25] This dispute is contradicted by an earlier incident. An illegal outpost of a settlement was demolished in accordance with the Israeli government.[26] However, this incident is in compliance with a speech held by Netanyahu in front of the US Congress. As Netanyahu said:

"The status of the settlements will be decided only in negotiations. But we must also be honest. So I am saying today something that should be said publicly by anyone serious about peace. In any peace agreement that ends the conflict, some settlements will end up beyond Israel's borders. The precise delineation of those borders must be negotiated. We will be very generous on the size of a future Palestinian state. But as President Obama

---

[22] See Chaim Levinson, "Ulpana developer lied and told residents that outpost was built on WZO, not Palestinian land," Haaretz, http://www.haaretz.com/news/diplomacy-defense/ulpana-developer-lied-and-told-residents-that-outpost-was-built-on-wzo-not-palestinian-land-1.430640. [05/24/2012].

[23] Cf E. Hausen, "Gericht: Abriss illegaler Siedlungsgebäude bis Anfang Juli," Israelnetz.com, http://www.israelnetz.com/themen/innenpolitik/artikel-innenpolitik/datum/2012/05/08/gericht-abriss-illegaler-siedlungsgebaeude-bis-anfang-juli/. [05/24/2012].

[24] Cf Moshe Arens, "It's wrong to push out Israeli settlers, even if its legal," Haaretz, http://www.haaretz.com/opinion/it-s-wrong-to-push-out-israeli-settlers-even-if-its-legal-1.427420. [05/24/2012].

[25] See Haaretz-Editorial, "Ulpana can't turn into a memorial for Israel's rule of law," Haaretz, http://www.haaretz.com/opinion/ulpana-can-t-turn-into-a-memorial-for-israel-s-rule-of-law-1.427041. [05/24/2012].

[26] See Haaretz-Editorial, "Netanyahu did the right thing by clearing Hebron outpost," Haaretz, http://www.haaretz.com/opinion/netanyahu-did-the-right-thing-by-clearing-hebron-outpost-1.422668. [05/24/2012].

said, the border will be different than the one that existed on June 4, 1967. Israel will not return to the indefensible lines of 1967."[27]

In other words, Netanyahu was willing and presumably still is to give up settlements for a peace agreement with the Palestinians. This may be proofed through several events, in which illegal outposts of settlements were destroyed or settlers were treated rigorously.[28] Nonetheless, there are also arguments that contradict Netanyahu's willingness to stop settlement-constructions. In an issue of *Time Magazine* of May 28, 2012 an article about Netanyahu was published, which cites the Prime Minister: "Peace treaties don't guarantee peace,"[29] – in consequence he refrained from freezing the actual settlement policy, which would include restricting the building of new houses in existing settlements and an absolute non-acceptance of illegal settlements or outposts of settlements. In the end, one has to keep in mind that settlements are illegal, as they violate the UN Security Council Resolution 242[30] passed on November 22, 1967.[31]

---

[27] Binyamin Netanyahu, "Speech by PM Netanyahu to a Joint Meeting of the U.S. Congress," Israel Prime Minister's Office, http://www.pmo.gov.il/PMOEng/-Communication/PMSpeaks/speechcongress240511.htm. [05/24/2012].

[28] See, e.g, Chaim Levinson, "IDF demolishes third illegal West Bank outpost this week," Haaretz, http://www.haaretz.com/news/national/idf-demolishes-third-illegal-west-bank-outpost-this-week-1.406870. [05/25/2012]; and D. Nowak, "Netanjahu gegen illegale Siedlungsaußenposten," Israelnetz, http://www.israelnetz.com-/themen/innenpolitik/artikel-innenpolitik/datum/2011/11/08/netanjahu-gegen-illegale-siedlungsaussenposten/. [05/25/2012].
Another remarkable event may be seen in the reaction of Netanyahu and his Defense Minister Ehud Barak. They agreed to call young and radical settlers a terrorist group. These settlers named themselves 'Hilltop Youth' (*Noar Hagivaot*).
See JPost.com-Staff, "Barak: Consider 'hilltop youth' a terror group," Jerusalem Post, http://www.jpost.com/Defense/Article.aspx?id=249390. [05/25/2012]; and Peter Münch, "Gefahr für Demokratie und Sicherheit," Süddeutsche Zeitung, http:/-/www.sueddeutsche.de/politik/gewalt-juedischer-siedler-gefahr-fuer-demokratie-und-sicherheit-1.1235272. [05/25/2012].

[29] Citation taken from Richard Stengel, "Bibi's Choice," *Time* 179, no. 21 (2012): 26.

[30] Excerpt of the Resolution: "[The Security Council] *affirms* that the fulfillment of Charter principles requires ... the application of both the following principles: (a) withdrawal of Israeli armed forces from territories occupied in the recent conflict; (b) termination of all claims or states of belligerency and respect for and acknowledgment of the sovereignty, ... free from threats or acts of force; [Emphasis in original.]" United Nations Security Council, Resolution 242, Rabinovich and Reinharz, *Israel in the Middle East - Documents and Readings on Society, Politics, and Foreign Relations, Pre-1948 to the Present*, 242.

Furthermore, unrelated to the aforesaid, it is planned to install a *United Nations Human Rights Council* (UNHRC) "to investigate the issue of Israeli settlements in the West Bank."[32] In Israel, it was received as an insult as commentaries reveal. "We will not permit members of the human rights council to visit Israel and our ambassador has been instructed to not even answer phone calls[, a representative said.] The secretariat of the human rights council and Nabi Pilawai sparked this process by establishing an international investigative committee on settlements, and we will thus not work with them anymore and will not appear before the council."[33] The ambassador himself was enraged stating in a meeting of the UNHRC: "The resolution [of the UNHRC to investigate in the West Bank] is unjustified and counterproductive. It will add tension and bitterness to an already explosive situation. This Council, by its own doing, is adding fuel to a fire which is [Israel's] duty to try and extinguish. Today will not be remembered as a glorious day for this Council."[34] The reaction of the US ambassador Charles O. Blaha is in harmony with the Israeli one: "We [the United States] remain committed to achieving a real, lasting peace between Palestinians and Israelis, a goal that requires both parties to take meaningful steps. The U.S. position on settlements is clear and has not changed: we do not accept the legitimacy of continued Israeli settlement activity. The status quo is not sustainable for either the Israelis or the Palestinians."[35] Nevertheless, as another commentary of *Haaretz* declares: "In any case, no UN inves-

---

[31] Cf Eldar and Zertal, *Lords of the Land - The War Over Israel's Settlements in the Occupied Territories, 1967 - 2007*: 56.

[32] Barak Ravid, "U.S. pressing UN Human Rights Commissioner to put off West Bank settlements probe," Haaretz, http://www.haaretz.com/blogs/diplomania/u-s-pressing-un-human-rights-commissioner-to-put-off-west-bank-settlements-probe-1.427744. [05/24/2012].

[33] Citation taken from Barak Ravid, "Israel cuts contact with UN rights council, to protest settlements probe," Haaretz, http://www.haaretz.com/news/diplomacy-defense/-israel-cuts-contact-with-un-rights-council-to-protest-settlements-probe-1.420786. [05/24/2012].

[34] Aharon Leshno-Yaar, "Statement to the UNHRC by Israel's Ambassador Aharon Leshno-Yaar," Israel Ministry of Foreign Affairs, http://www.mfa.gov.il/MFA-/Foreign+Relations/Israel+and+the+UN/Issues/Response_UNHRC_commission_settlements_22-Mar-2012. [05/24/2012].

[35] Citation taken from Charles O. Blaha, "U.S. Strongly Objects to HRC's Creation of One-sided Fact Finding Mission on Israeli Settlements," Permanent Mission of the United States of America in Geneva, http://geneva.usmission.gov/2012/03/22/-israeli-settlements/. [05/25/2012].

tigative committee is needed to understand that the West Bank belongs to another people and its lands are not available to a Jewish and democratic state."[36]

One can derive from that that the settlements are currently as hotly debated as always; presumably it will continue in this way, in spite of withdrawals from the Sinai Peninsula and the Gaza Strip.

2. Gush Emunim

Gush Emunim was founded in February 1974[37] by a group of religious Zionists, who were all settlers in the wake of the movement. The 'members'[38] saw it as their religious duty to bring an organization into life that defends the concerns of settlers. Participants of the first meeting were Yoel Bin-Nun, Zevulun Hammer, a member of the NRP, R. Moshe Levinger of Kiryat Arba, R. Haim Druckman, who had accompanied R. Levinger together with Eliezer Waldman to Hebron. There were further Gershon Shafat and Hannan Porat of Kfar Etzion. All of them met at Bin-Nun's home in the settlement Alon Shvut. Gershon Shafat mentioned to R. Druckman that there is a "need to do something [in order] to get the wagon of the depressed that is stuck in the vale of tears up the mountain."[39] They decided to meet more often, because the actual situation demanded it, and came to the conclusion, with another member of the NRP (National Religious Party), Yehuda Ben-Meir, that there has to be an organization that supports the 'cry of Samaria and Judea' (the West Bank) for more Jews. After this the founding fathers of Gush Emunim, as named above, recruited new 'members' who varied between relatives, friends, classmates, and the like.[40]

The so-called founding myth of Gush Emunim followed in the Sebastia settlement over a year later in November 1975. The Elon Moreh group, in

---

[36] Haaretz-Editorial, "UN probe must take West Bank out of Israeli hands," Haaretz, http://www.haaretz.com/opinion/un-probe-must-take-west-bank-out-of-israeli-hands-1.421844. [05/24/2012].

[37] Cf Lilly Weissbrod, "Gush Emunim ideology — from religious doctrine to political action," *Middle Eastern Studies* 18, no. 3 (1982): 266.

[38] There exists no official declaration for Gush Emunim's foundation. It does not see itself as an organization.

[39] Citation taken from Eldar and Zertal, *Lords of the Land - The War Over Israel's Settlements in the Occupied Territories, 1967 - 2007*: 204.

[40] Cf ibid., 204-05.

this case the spearhead of Gush Emunim,[41] had already tried to take place in Sebastia seven times. However, every time the settlers were evacuated in violent clashes by IDF soldiers. The eighth time Gush Emunim planned to occupation of Sebastia in minutiae and like a military operation; therefore they occupied Sebastia this time. More than a few thousand ascended the mountain. They arrived with their families, including small children and babies, and were religious or secular, and all *couleurs* of Zionists showed up. The devotees were partly animated through an advertisement of Gush Emunim:

"We call upon you, who see how the Jewish people is abandoned to the hatchets of the Palestinian Liberation Organization in the corridors of the UN, suffering the insult of portions of the land of Israel that are empty of Jews, seeing the government of Israel in its weakness and impotence in face of the plan for the Palestinian state that is simmering in Samaria: Come with us. Get out of the house, put off all your business and join the great move of the Jewish people that is returning home."[42]

Other participants in this 'showdown' were Menachem Begin and Ariel Sharon, Yitzchak Rabin's advisor at the time. They led over 400 supporters to Sebastia.

The victory over the Israeli government was accompanied by the song '*Utzu eytza vetufar*' (Take counsel together) – it became the anthem of Gush Emunim and Sebastia. The event was covered by journalists and put Gush Emunim in the center of attention in the Israeli public. The government of Rabin, who himself literally hated all about the settlement movement, was forced to allow the settlers to remain in Sebastia, at least for a short time in a military camp. Gush Emunim publically proclaimed victory over the Rabin government. In the end the government collapsed over the discussion about demands and questions of the settlement.[43]

Long before the government resignation, Rabin sent Defense Minister Shimon Peres to the settlers to negotiate. Peres, however, sided with the settlers.

"It was not just Gush Emunim, ... inside the camp (in Sebastia) there were people from the established agricultural settlements and kibbutzim of

---

[41] "The two groups merged, agreeing that the movement would not be affiliated with any political party and their joint mode of action was decided – 'actual, physical settlement in the territory.'" ibid.

[42] Citation taken from ibid., 43.

[43] Cf ibid., 43-46, 183-87.

all stripes. ... A democratic regime has to respect the law, but there are laws, and there are very many of them, about which the government is authorized by the legislator to use its judgment as to how to enforce them. The law does not blindly and automatically command the government to use it (the law) alone. ... Even though the law says that every individual must be conscripted in the IDF the defense minister, not because of provisions that exist in the law but *for reasons that reach into the very soul of the nation*, exempts certain people from conscription. ... In my opinion, I have been given the authority, non in an unknown situation but rather on the background of what is known, to manage the issue. As someone who does not scorn the desires and pressures of Gush Emunim – I think that they are good citizens and good settlers – I do not think that Gush Emunim should dictate policy to the government. [Emphasis in original.]"[44]

Peres' statement was aimed at the parliament in order to persuade it. In consequence the settlers were given more time to stay at Sebastia. Rabin did know that this was a waggly compromise and responded to it in the Knesset. "I see it as one of the most serious problems. ... Gush Emunim ... is threatening the democratic way of life in the state of Israel, and confronting it must be done on all levels. ... I have no illusion that with the agreement we ended the confrontation ... because the aim is to use lawbreaking to impose a way."[45] After all, Gush Emunim succeeded and the Sebastia settlement was built thus creating a founding myth.

After the collapse of the Rabin government and the formation of the Sebastia settlement, Menachem Begin succeeded Yitzchak Rabin. For the first time ever, the rightist party Likud came to power in Israel. "The 1977 Likud victory marked in a dramatic way the broadening of the range of difference in relevant political debate. ... There was a need of a new paradigm to describe Israeli society and politics, as the classic Zionist vision of the Jewish state – or at least its Labor Zionist version – became increasingly irrelevant. Such a new paradigm would need to encompass not only the emerging nationalist right but also the more assertive and visible religious communities, both Zionist and [Haredim] in Israel and in the occupied territories."[46] As seen in the statistics on the West Bank settlements, these flourished very fast and attracted many citizens. However, Begin got under

---

[44] Citation taken from ibid., 49.

[45] Citation taken from ibid., 50.

[46] Alan Dowty, *The Jewish State - A Century Later* (Berkeley, Los Angeles, London: University of California Press, 1998). 111.

pressure of the Carter administration which demanded more restriction in settlement policy of Israel. In consequence Begin advised Hannan Porat of Gush Emunim to establish only six new settlements instead of twelve as had originally been agreed. "While at one level Likud occupation policy tried to make renewed settlement difficult or impossible, at another level it sought to make a permanent Israeli role in the territories acceptable by developing as much de facto autonomy or self-rule on the local level as possible."[47] In answer to all this *tohu-wa-bohu* Gush Emunim threatened to nevertheless found twelve settlements. The prime minister was outraged. "Anyone who settles – will be removed by force!"[48]

Gush Emunim was not pleased with the current situation, but settlements were established as far as possible. A new dispute broke out over the peace agreement of Egypt, which included not only the dismantlement of settlements, but also a freeze of settlement construction for at least three months. In this controversy the prime minister was confronted with harsh phrases by Gush Emunim, which every prime minister had had to endure since the existence of Gush Emunim. "If we have to make the choice between you and the Land of Israel, then the Land of Israel is preferable."[49] Further he was called '*Judenrat*' of Yamit.[50]

During the dismantling of the Sinai settlements, the case of Elon Moreh surfaced. This was inspired by R. Zvi Yehuda Kook Jr., hundreds of settlers and devotees followed his 'battle' cry. They occupied a mountain and surrounded it with a fence. The occupiers announced that they loved the Land of Israel and that they would sabotage any agreement the government of Israel would sign to alter their current condition. Nonetheless, all people were evacuated by force. Gush Emunim won the battle, as the government gave way to Elon Moreh, but not on the mountain they had temporarily taken. The settlement was, however, founded on private Palestinian land; even in opposition to many ministers who claimed that one must not confiscate private land of Palestinians in a densely Arab-populated area only for a settlement. Land was given to the settlers and Elon Moreh established. Protests by the Israeli opposition, Palestinians, international organizations, the US administration, and the American Jewry immediately followed. One

---

[47] Ibid., 219.

[48] Citation taken from Eldar and Zertal, *Lords of the Land - The War Over Israel's Settlements in the Occupied Territories, 1967 - 2007*: 57.

[49] Citation taken from ibid., 62.

[50] Cf ibid., 75.

of the next steps in this heated conflict was that the Palestinian landowners took the case to the Supreme Court. The reason that the settlement was not a security matter for the State of Israel, but a matter of faith and obedience to G-d for eternity, led the court to judge that the settlement had to be dismantled and the land returned to its owners within thirty days. Gush Emunim was shocked by the decision and refused to leave the place. Again, the army had to intervene and force the settlers from the mountain. At least for the moment, the government of Israel emerged as the winner.[51]

The acts of Jewish terrorism in Israel left bloody stains on the otherwise clean record of Gush Emunim. Menachem Livni, one of the terrorists, was a disciple of R. Levinger. The interrogation of Livni revealed that R. Levinger supported the plan of terrorist attacks in a 'general way' and R. Meir Yehuda Getz and R. Haim Sabato directly supported the plan. Nonetheless all of them denied any connections to the terrorist.[52] But, Livni and his terror companions, however, strongly discredited Gush Emunim. In a series of further terrorist attacks on Palestinian mayors, Gush Emunim and settlement leaders responded that they opposed such terrorism, as it harmed "Israeli statehood in its current embodiment," [53] as Shlomo Aviner, a dovish Gush member, claimed.

Gush Emunim had accomplished its mission to establish settlements in the West Bank. This movement was active in the Sinai Peninsula, Gaza Strip and the Golan Heights, with involvement in the latter to the present day, though the bloc did not have the power to withstand the dismantlement of the Peninsula. The Oslo Accords (in the eyes of Gush Emunim the Accords had been an attack on them by Rabin) and the evacuation of the settlements in the Gaza Strip could not be stopped by an intervention of Gush Emunim. But since then, "Gush Emunim has been weakened to the degree that in recent years it no longer functions as a distinct organization with an established system of decision making."[54] It seems that "it lacks an

---

[51] Cf ibid., 63-70.

[52] Cf ibid., 76-79.

[53] Citation taken from ibid., 83.

[54] Eliezer Don-Yehiya, "Two Movements of Messianic Awakening and Their Attitude to Halacha, Nationalism, and Democracy: The Cases of Habad and Gush Emunim," in *Tolerance, Dissent, and Democracy - Philosophical, Historical, and Halakhic Perspectives*, ed. Moshe Sokol (Northvale: Jason Aronson Inc., 2002), 266.

authoritative leadership with the ability to arrive decisions binding on members of the movement."[55]

The *raison d'être* of Gush Emunim is of a different *couleur* as one might expect, when only taking a short glimpse at the matter. At first I present the thinking of R. Abraham Isaac Hacohen Kook, the first Ashkenazi Chief Rabbi of Palestine. His thoughts were interpreted and taught by R. Zvi Yehuda Kook in the yeshiva *Merkaz Harav* in Jerusalem. R. Kook Jr. was the only one who was allowed to interpret the thoughts of R. Kook Sr., or put another way: R. Kook Jr. was authorized by his father, because the younger understood the 'inner feelings' of his father's heart.[56] "While Rabbi Avraham Itzhak Hacohen Kook undoubtedly built a major intellectual system, his ideo-theology was not based on logical rigor and empirical verification. Instead elements of faith, secrecy, unearthly intuition, supernatural illumination, mystery, and paradox have always been essential components of his thought;"[57] as Ehud Sprinzak introduces the *Weltanschauung* of R. Kook Sr. As we know of the ideology of the Habad movement, it has not to be logic or non-paradox, as long as it is working.

The older R. Kook was convinced of *geulah* (redemption) brought by Messiah (*b'ikvata d'meshiah*) as well as were many other Jews on earth; however, he was not in full accord with the interpretation of *geulah*. R. Kook Sr. believed that one has to immigrate to Palestine and not remain in the diaspora (*galut*). According to the interpretation of *the Rebbe* about *galut/geulah* as discussed above, one has only to add one Aleph letter in the middle and the meaning totally changes. In other words, the older R. Kook supported the way Theodor Herzl (b. 1860 – d. 1904), the founder of the Zionism movement and a secular Jew, took to proclaim immigration to Palestine for Jews.

Nonetheless, beside the way of Zionism, religious Jews did not believe in such *'apikursut'* (heresy), because a Jew is not supposed to immigrate to Palestine before Messiah is coming, bolstered with several reasons:

---

[55] Eliezer Don-Yehiya, "The Book and the Sword - The Nationalist Yeshivot and Political Radicalism in Israel," in *Accounting For Fundamentalisms - The Dynamic Character of Movements*, ed. R. Scott Appleby and Martin E. Marty (Chicago, London: The University of Chicago Press, 1994), 286.

[56] Cf Eldar and Zertal, *Lords of the Land - The War Over Israel's Settlements in the Occupied Territories, 1967 - 2007*: 191.

[57] Ehud Sprinzak, *The Ascendence of Israel's Radical Right* (New York: Oxford University Press, 1991). 110.

"Firstly, man must not interfere with God's will, or compete with Him. Secondly, God was in exile, together with the Jewish people, so that a return to Palestine would be useless unless God returned to the Holy Land. Since that would occur only with the coming of the Messiah, a return of the Jewish people to Palestine would not bring the people nearer to God and would not hasten salvation. Thirdly, suffering in the diaspora was a duty imposed by God on the people of Israel, and was a means to purification and perfection. Therefore, 'hastening the end' was a sin."[58]

R. Kook Sr.'s opinion differed, as he claimed there is a difference in Jewish suffering. There is material suffering and physical suffering, and these two diverge in their meaning. On the one hand, material suffering, the impoverishment and the persecution existing since thousands of years, did not endanger Judaism, but the physical one, on the other hand, had been in existence since the assimilation of the 19th and 20th centuries – the ultimate danger for Jewish existence. Therefore, it is of the highest importance for a revival of the Jewish religion and a renewal of Jewish unity of its own people to emigrate. In Palestine they would found their own nation, and nationhood, to name it, has been an essential part of the Jewish religion since the covenant between G-d and Moses had been declared.

Jewish nationalism is also not inconsistent with the Messianic vision of international peace and a union of all different peoples. It even supports a messianic version as soon as the Jewish people sets an example of perfection and shows how international peace may be possible. Further, Jews can only embody holiness when united to one strong people; this can only be reached through Zionism, which in fact for R. Kook Sr. is the manifestation of Jewish nationalism itself.[59] Zionism is the new ground the Jewish people

---

[58] Weissbrod, "Gush Emunim ideology — from religious doctrine to political action," 267.

[59] "The three official parties in the life of our nation: one, the Orthodox party, as we are accustomed to call it, which carries the banner of the holy, pitches stridently, jealously, bitterly for Torah and commandments, faith, and all that is holy in Israel; the second, the new Nationalist party, campaigns for all the aspirations of the nationalist tendency, which comprises much of the pure naturalism of the nation, which desires to renew its national life, after it was so long hidden within due to the violence of the bitter exile [galut or all non-Jewish countries], and much of that which is absorbed from other nations, which it desires to recognize as positive inasmuch as it deems it fitting for itself (the Jewish People) as well; the third is the liberal party, which not so long ago carried the banner of Enlightenment, whose influence is still great in wide circles, does not fit into the nationalist scheme and seeks the universal human content of the Enlightenment, culture, ethics, and so forth. It is understood

has to break, as it recreates idealism and idealism is of absolute importance and needed to re-establish the belief in G-d in the assimilated Jewry due to the mystical union between the Jewish people and the Bible.

G-d H-mself chose the land Palestine for the Jewish people to settle; it therefore is only consequent to now go back to the Holy Land. The older R. Kook was convinced that all the secular, assimilated, or even atheistic Zionists, who were disciples of Herzl, will come back to Jewish belief. It is necessary to be tolerant toward all Jews who partake in this venture. In the view of R. Kook Sr. the 'shell' of Zionism will crack in the end and an inner 'spiritual light' reveal itself as an expression of religious revival.[60] But Palestine has to be settled first, this is a central commandment, as there the Jewish people would become once more an instrument of Divine Inspiration for the rest of mankind – 'the old will be renewed and the new will be sanctified.' The return to Palestine rather serves for a spiritual independence than a national one. [61]

In the teachings of R. Kook Sr., he proposed, in contrast to the Jewish orthodox world, immigration to Palestine. Palestine would not be *galut*, as many other Jews claim – it is *the* haven for Jews. Jewish faith would be renewed there and Jewish unity would come to life again. As the older R. Kook emphasized, the physical suffering of Jews exposed to assimilation is a danger for Jews.

His son and only authorized interpreter of his father's teachings translated the main claims of *aliyah* to Palestine, to immigration to the West Bank, the Sinai Peninsula, the Gaza Strip, and the Golan Heights. In the words of R. Kook Jr.: "All this land is ours, absolutely, belonging to all of us; it is non-transferable to others even in part [because] it was promised to

---

that in a healthy state there is a need for these three forces together, and we must always aspire to come to this healthy state, in which these three forces together will rein in all of their plentitude and goodness, in a whole, harmonious state in which there is neither lack nor superfluity, for the Holy, the Nation and Man [these represents the *Holy Trinity* of R. Kook Sr.: the Holy is the Torah, the Nation is meant to be Palestine or the Land of Israel, and Man is the *am Yisrael*, the Jewry], will cleave together in a love lofty and practical." Benjamin Brown, "Rabbi A. Y. Kook on Ideological Diversity and Unity," in *The Blackwell Reader in Judaism*, ed. Jacob Neusner and Alan J. Avery-Peck (Cornwall: Blackwall Publishers Ltd, 2001), 240.

[60] Cf Don-Yehiya, "The Book and the Sword - The Nationalist Yeshivot and Political Radicalism in Israel," 270.

[61] Cf Weissbrod, "Gush Emunim ideology — from religious doctrine to political action," 267-68.

us by God, Creator of the World."[62] R. Kook Jr.'s starting point was the ideology of his father applied to the newly-occupied land; and with this background, the younger Kook went on to build his own version of a 'new' religious Zionism. His father had claimed that "the End has already awoken, the third coming has begun."[63] R. Kook Jr. went further: "The End is being revealed before our very eyes, and there can be no doubt or question that would detract from our joy and gratitude to the Redeemer of Israel. ... The End is here."[64] This citation from *Lord of the Lands* is directly linked to a sentence of Lilly Weissbrod, in which she mentions that R. Kook Sr. was convinced that with the return of the Jewish people to Palestine the coming of the Messiah would be heralded (*b'ikvata d'meshiah*), but his son went further and set the time of redemption into the present of his own existence; a settler corroborated his points stating: "My husband and I are convinced that we are living in a most fateful period. If we prove to be exclusive proprietors of Eretz Israel, of the parts we have already managed to liberate, it will hasten redemption."[65] Not only was this substantiated by the settler, R. Kook Jr. did it himself, as he preached: "No, it is not we who are forcing the End, but the End that is forcing us!"[66]

Therefore, any withdrawal from Gaza Strip, Sinai Peninsula, or, in the worst case, Judea and Samaria (the West Bank) would be cursed by G-d. As a part of this redemption would be the conquest and settlement of the land. "This is dictated by divine politics, and no earthly politics can supersede it."[67] It is no wonder to hear statements of Gush Emunim spokesmen: "Settlement is above the law"[68] or "We recognise the existence of the State of

---

[62] Citation taken from ibid., 269.

[63] Citation taken from Eldar and Zertal, *Lords of the Land - The War Over Israel's Settlements in the Occupied Territories, 1967 - 2007*: 193.

[64] Citation taken from ibid.

[65] Citation taken from Weissbrod, "Gush Emunim ideology — from religious doctrine to political action," 269.

[66] Citation taken from Eldar and Zertal, *Lords of the Land - The War Over Israel's Settlements in the Occupied Territories, 1967 - 2007*: 202.

[67] Citation taken from ibid., 210.

[68] Such phrases have always been a problem for the average settler, who has no relation to Gush Emunim whatsoever, who settles in fact only there because of their belief in Greater Israel. Average settlers want to be seen as a part of the modern Israeli society and not to be meshed with the fanatics of Gush Emunim. Though Israeli society sees most of the settlers as religious fanatics, many settlers only claim their rights to believe in their own way. But they would rather follow decisions of the government than being against them. Cf David Newman, "From Hitnachalut to Hitnatkut: The

Israel, of course we do. But we say that Eretz Israel overrides all Knesset (parliament) law."[69] Kook repeatedly taught that the occupied territories are rightful property of the Jewish people. "Once and for all, it is clear and absolute that there are no 'Arab territories' or 'Arab lands' here, but only the lands of Israel, the eternal heritage of our forefathers to which others have come upon which they have built without our permission and in our absence."[70] Arabs had, in the ideology of Rav Kook Jr., a number of given roles; the Arabs had to remind the Jewish people, which tends to forget and even to adopt foreign cultures, of being unique and chosen by G-d; and the Arabs had to keep the Jewish people in 'constant war' to preserve the 'unity' of the Jewish people. Arabs have been degraded by Gush Emunim to something that is no sovereign human being with identical and unalienable rights.[71]

In consequence, stubbornness of the Holy Land and its relation to the Jewish people, made R. Kook Jr. extend the tolerance of his father solely relying on Jewish pioneers, who may be atheistic, to the Jewry on the whole earth. The younger Kook was cited, "I do not accept these concepts of religious/non-religious ... the Jewish people is one unit and there are thousands of degrees of Jewishness."[72] Furthermore, R. Kook Jr. demanded a *pan-Israeliness.*' Eventually, "there is a spark of holiness [in every Jew], which even if it is hidden must be awakened, developed and brought close."[73]

In conclusion there stood a 'Holy Trinity', consisting of *Eretz Yisrael* (the land of Israel, this time including West Bank, Sinai Peninsula, Gaza Strip, and the Golan Heights), the people of Israel, *Am Yisrael* (the world Jewry), and the Torah of Israel,[74] which connected all the aforesaid. This 'Holy

---

Impact of Gush Emunim and the Settlement Movement on Israeli Politics and Society," *Israel Studies* 10, no. 3 (2005): 199.

[69] Citations taken from Weissbrod, "Gush Emunim ideology — from religious doctrine to political action," 269.

[70] Citation taken from Eldar and Zertal, *Lords of the Land - The War Over Israel's Settlements in the Occupied Territories, 1967 - 2007*: 212.

[71] Cf ibid., 218.

[72] Citation taken from Weissbrod, "Gush Emunim ideology — from religious doctrine to political action," 269.

[73] Citation taken from Eldar and Zertal, *Lords of the Land - The War Over Israel's Settlements in the Occupied Territories, 1967 - 2007*: 206.

[74] Cf Sprinzak, *The Ascendence of Israel's Radical Right*: 112-13.

Trinity' was from its beginning on also part of the ideology of Gush Emunim.

Out of the reason that it is almost impossible to separate the ideologies of Rav Kook Jr.[75] and Gush Emunim, I begin with the latter's ideology. Firstly, Gush Emunim was born out of the ideology of R. Kook Jr. and thus their ideologies overlap. Gush Emunim The bloc of faithful members adhered and literally willingly exposed themselves to the homilies of *Merkaz Harav*, with R. Kook Jr. as its main preacher; albeit the younger Rav Kook was not involved in all the activities of the bloc.[76] The younger Kook died, while the Sinai *hitnatkut* happened.

The bloc adopted the procedure of Kook's yeshiva and never established a democratic system in their movement. It rather reigned with "a small and self-selected hard-core leadership,"[77] and had a far reaching periphery which was easy to activate. As the bloc was committed to the preaching of younger R. Kook they did obey his idea of tolerance for other Jews – therefore the bloc was never strictly orthodox (only partly ultra-Orthodox), but many nationalists also did found their place in the bloc. "For Gush Emunim, secular support for their cause was attributed to ... mystical factors. ... At the mystical level, Gush Emunim attributed the support of the secular elements in terms of Rabbi Kook [Sr.] ideology, inasmuch as he had argued that all of the secular Zionist pioneers had demonstrated an inner (often unconscious) spark of holiness by virtue of the fact that they were building up the Land of Israel which would eventually bring about redemption [*geulah*]."[78] Further, the openness to secularity was declared by the older Kook, that means that all the for-the-moment-atheists will see when the state will flower out, that all their intentions of national rebirth and even

---

[75] A quite interesting note is that the younger Kook gave Menachem Begin his blessing. Begin then went to the Western Wall to say a prayer. Usually a new prime minister goes to the respective Chief Rabbi of Israel. Further, Begin was known to be only a moderately observant Jew, but he went even to the spiritual vanguard of Gush Emunim. Begin, at first, was a new supporter of the bloc, then became the *Kapo* due to the peace treaty with Egypt and the withdrawal of the Sinai Peninsula included therein, but with the war against Lebanon (also according to Gush Emunim, which relied on Genesis 15, a part of Greater Israel) Begin became a *real* Jew again. Cf Weissbrod, "Gush Emunim ideology — from religious doctrine to political action," 265. And cf Sprinzak, *The Ascendence of Israel's Radical Right*: 113-14.

[76] Cf Sprinzak, *The Ascendence of Israel's Radical Right*: 151.

[77] Ibid., 108.

[78] Newman, "From Hitnachalut to Hitnatkut: The Impact of Gush Emunim and the Settlement Movement on Israeli Politics and Society," 197-98.

their *aliyah* was just based on their religiosity. Without knowing it, they had suppressed their religiosity. Finally, the atheists, according to Rav Kook Sr., will find their 'Holy Spark.' All commandments will be logical for them and absolutely natural to observe.[79] Again and again the Kook's *raison d'être* hovers over almost every event of Gush Emunim. Gush Emunim Orthodox Jews saw as form of 'missionary work' to show tolerance towards even fractionally atheistic Jews. The ambition and the preaching at the beginning of the bloc of the younger R. Kook, later through various other rabbis, was hoped by religious bloc adherents to be an example of G-dly power indwelling into the atheists, therefore it may help to convert unreligious nationalists to bring them back to the religiosity of the faithful of the bloc – *new religious Zionism*.[80]

The tolerance for non-religious, *hiloni* Jews, maybe even atheistic Jews, preached and shown by both Kooks and by the Gush Emunim did not imply tolerance toward gentiles and antipathy toward Arabs. Arabs are not enemies of Jews; they are deadly foes, proclaimed the settler David Rosenzweig. At first, the bloc equated Arabs with Nazis. After a while it was more common to say that Arabs are much worse than the Nazis. Rosenzweig went on with his blind wrath and hatred toward Arabs, as the situation of deadly foes is "a situation of struggle in which there are no compromises, for life and death. The aggressive side, that is the deadly foe, has as his aim to destroy, to kill and to exterminate."[81] R. Kook Jr. gave Arabs an inhuman role (see above); it is therefore no wonder, to read statements of his disciples or other rabbis, influenced by Kook's yeshiva *Merkaz Harav*, who continued to hate Arabs. Yaakov Medan, for example, wrote: "The Holy One, blessed be He, imposed the Six-Day Way on us, to

---

[79] Cf Eldar and Zertal, *Lords of the Land - The War Over Israel's Settlements in the Occupied Territories, 1967 - 2007*: 195.

[80] Cf Weissbrod, "Gush Emunim ideology — from religious doctrine to political action," 270.

[81] Eldar and Zertal, *Lords of the Land - The War Over Israel's Settlements in the Occupied Territories, 1967 - 2007*: 219. It is important to add that *deadly foe* was used only twice in Jewish history. At first for the tribe of the Amalekites, an ancient foe of the Jewry, which G-d commanded to be destroyed. Later it was used for the Nazis. Haim Tzuria stated: "In each generation we have those who rise up to wipe us out, therefore each generation has its own Amalek. The Amalekism of our generation expresses itself in the extremely deep hatred of the Arabs to our national renaissance in the land of our forefathers." Citation taken from Sprinzak, *The Ascendence of Israel's Radical Right*: 123.

cleanse the domain of Abraham, Isaac and Jacob of the evil regime that ruled there." According to Dov Lior of Kiryat Arbat the best Arab is a dead Arab. Another settler, Moshe Ben-Yosef (Hager) argued: "Evacuating the land of its inhabitants is a Zionist goal of the first rank, no less and perhaps even more than settling the land with Jewish inhabitants." In Gush Emunim the slogan 'No rights for the Arabs to the Land of Israel.' was common practice. The Arabs possessing land, would only lead to the following consequence: "our right itself does not exist and we [the Jewish people] are all war criminals that are sentenced to death by a court for crimes against humanity."[82]

The hatred was not limited to the Arabs alone, it went against all gentiles. *antisemitism* did not play such as intensive role as it had played for Herzl, who hence founded the Zionistic movement. Neither did the older Rav Kook want peace or normalization with gentiles, or antisemites, nor did Gush Emunim wish for a normalization of its relationship with the gentile world.[83]

"Any framework or international whose resolutions imply the humiliation of the honor of Israel has no right to exist and we consequently do not belong there[, but to Eretz Israel in its *Hashlema* (Greater Israel) form]. We must leave that organization and wait for the day when the honor of Israel would rise again and the truth among the nations will be uncovered."[84]

This hatred is based on Security Council decisions and the various problems the State of Israel faced. Especially the Yom Kippur War of 1973 was a hit in the face of the settlers (Gush Emunim was shortly afterwards founded) and the yeshiva *Merkaz Harav*. This war was perceived as "the final attempt of the Gentiles to stop the coming of the redemption of the Jews. It was a struggle against God Himself."[85]

---

[82] All citations taken from Eldar and Zertal, *Lords of the Land - The War Over Israel's Settlements in the Occupied Territories, 1967 - 2007*: 218-19.

[83] A side-note, which has to be added, is that Rav Shach, the *Lituanei* leader of the party *Torah ha-degel*, and presumably one of the most intense haters of the Habad movement, insists that Jews should avoid trusting gentiles or even relying on them. Though, his opinion toward Arabs is in contrast to that, as he opposes any militant or harsh policies against Arabs. He claims that Israel must allow territorial concessions for the sake of peace. Cf Don-Yehiya, "Two Movements of Messianic Awakening and Their Attitude to Halacha, Nationalism, and Democracy: The Cases of Habad and Gush Emunim," 287.

[84] Citation taken from Sprinzak, *The Ascendence of Israel's Radical Right*: 115.

[85] Ibid., 116.

After the death of Rav Kook Jr., Gush Emunim broke apart into two blocs over issues of its ideology. R. Yisrael Ariel is located on the hardline-hawkish side. He showed sympathy for the 'Jewish Underground' and the terror attacks which were operated by them. The *Weltanschauung* of R. Ariel surfaces especially in his arguments explaining why he shows sympathy for Jewish terrorism. The State of Israel is a democracy, but has never been Jewish, because, following his argumentation, Judaism needs to have 'the Kingdom of Israel' – *malkhut yisrael*. "When prophecy will reappear in Israel, namely when the Holy One, blessed be He, reveals His will, then government in Israel will be based on monarchy, not on democracy."[86] Similar arguments were posted by his Gush friend Yehuda Etzion, who was even involved in 'Jewish Underground' terrorism.

Gush Emunim also had dovish sides, which were shown by R. Zvi Tau, who had much influence in Kook's yeshiva *Merkaz Harav*. R. Tau opposed any use of illegal and violent methods adopted by Gush Emunim in the dismantlement of Yamit in 1982. Tau's argumentation contained, inter alia, that even if it may have wrong been by the Likud government of the early 1980's to give up settlements in the Peninsula, it cannot be right to oppose it, too. In a homily of R. Tau, he relied on his mentor, R. Kook Jr.:

"Rav Zvi Yehuda determined that the people are not with us and therefore we must cease our efforts. The men of action of Gush Emunim didn't agree and our paths parted. There is no mandate for five thousand people (in Yamit) to coerce the Jewish people, to revolt against the spirit of the nation ... this is a revolt against the kingship of God."[87]

In fact, it is possible without difficulties to find resentment toward violent forms in the circles of Gush Emunim. Professor Hillel Weiss, who originally was a very extreme settler, he realigned his view in 1980:

"We cannot expel the Arabs from Judea and Samaria, just at this stage we cannot build the Temple [the Third Temple, which is the wish of every messianic orientated Jew]. ... It is not just that we cannot, we do not want to! An attitude toward the Arab individual, his human liberties and his property, is an inseparable part of my worldview. Even an enemy is a hu-

---

[86] Giora Goldberg and Efraim Ben-Zadok, "Gush Emunim in the West Bank," *Middle Eastern Studies* 22, no. 1 (1986): 60.

[87] Don-Yehiya, "Two Movements of Messianic Awakening and Their Attitude to Halacha, Nationalism, and Democracy: The Cases of Habad and Gush Emunim," 301.

man being, as long as he does not express in action his desire to harm me as a Jew in the Land of Israel."[88]

Prof. Weiss was not the only to hold this opinion toward a more human relationship with neighbors, but also Hagai Ben-Artzi. He stated that Gush Emunim will not only be judged according to its success in consideration of settlements, but also in consideration of its moral attitude toward Arabs. "Yes, we nationalist Jews believe in the right of the Jewish people to return to its homeland ... but we are also Jews, whose heritage is replete with respect and love for every human being who was created in God's image." One of the founding members of Gush Emunim was considering Arabs on the side of the doves. "Any harm to Arabs who have not attacked us ... stands in utter contradiction not only to morality and law but also to the principles of Gush Emunim,"[89] argued Yoel Bin-Nun. His Gush friend Menachem Fruman even proposed relationships with Palestinians.

One further aspect of Gush Emunim has to be added, the praise of the IDF. The younger R. Kook wrote: "With the perfection of our military system ... the perfection of the essence of our rebirth is evident. We are no longer considered to be only 'The People of the Book.' Instead we are recognized as 'The People of God,' the holy people, for whom the Book and the sword together descended together from heaven."[90] The army, IDF, therefore played a big role in the procedure of Gush Emunim. R. Zvi Yehuda Kook took the politics of Israel for divine. One can derive from that that all the institutions of the state – especially the army – are to be honored. "Even 'non-Zionist' actions of the army required respect because they were deeds and an expression of the nation. The army's weapons, destined to defend life, underwent a transformation in Kook's thinking and became holy vessels themselves, elements in the theology of Redemption."[91] R. Kook Jr. gave a ritual and sacred meaning to all the objects of the IDF, be it its tanks, its artillery, or its aircraft. In Gush Emunim the army was praised and rose to a cultic status. "Enlistment in the army and service in elite combat units became Gush identity tags. ... The ideal of the pioneering and

---

[88] Citation taken from Eldar and Zertal, *Lords of the Land - The War Over Israel's Settlements in the Occupied Territories, 1967 - 2007*: 219-20.

[89] Citations taken from ibid., 220.

[90] Citation taken from Don-Yehiya, "The Book and the Sword - The Nationalist Yeshivot and Political Radicalism in Israel," 271.

[91] Eldar and Zertal, *Lords of the Land - The War Over Israel's Settlements in the Occupied Territories, 1967 - 2007*: 224-25.

pious settler was reinforced when it wore an IDF uniform."[92] The IDF knew that the religious Zionists, which included Gush Emunim settlers, respected them, wherefore the *Hesder* unit was established in the 1970s, which catered the religious obligations of the soldiers. As a result, *Hesder* was known for its highly motivated units. Nevertheless, these soldiers rather obeyed their rabbis than the commanders. "When army orders began to conflict with the religious teachings, most notably in the case of army involvement in the evacuation of settlements ... many soldiers ... refused to carry out the military orders of their superior officers."[93] The religious students had their problems to kill enemies: "I am convinced that our struggle is just and that justifies killing any man who comes to kill us ... I know my heart ached,"[94] said a religious soldier. Notwithstanding the soldier having killed enemies, he questioned his actions.

In summation, the bloc's *raison d'être* is based on the teachings of *Merkaz Harav*, the yeshiva of the Kooks. The main part of Gush's activity is to build new settlements, as it is embedded in their ideology of the 'Holy Trinity'. This means the Land of Israel, the actual soil, has to be populated with Jewish people, who not have to immediately become or already be religious. Though, at least in the intention of the Gush nucleus, they are to become religious after a while and the third part of the 'Holy Trinity', the Torah, will be praised.[95] However, the procedures to reach this level with a Jew on Jewish land of Greater Israel, who loves to study the Torah, vary.

On the one hand the radical way is to hate and kill Arabs, as they are no human beings, who never had any right to be on the land of the Jewish People. If necessary, terrorism is legitimate to reach the goal. On the other hand, the more licit way is to negotiate and connect to Palestinians, who are respected as human beings and neighbors. Further due to the respect for the laws of the State of Israel, even if it is not the Land of Israel, this way is preferred, therefore, it is a much smoother procedure to settle on the

---

[92] Ibid., 225.

[93] Newman, "From Hitnachalut to Hitnatkut: The Impact of Gush Emunim and the Settlement Movement on Israeli Politics and Society," 211.

[94] Citation taken from Weissbrod, "Gush Emunim ideology — from religious doctrine to political action," 272.

[95] Gush Emunim's nucleus has the intention to bring the Jewish flock to their national religious belief. It is therefore no wonder that the nucleus is called '*Hardal*' in Israel. This term is an amalgam of *Haredi* and *Leumi*; *Haredim* (ultra-Orthodox) and *Leumi* (National). Cf Newman, "From Hitnachalut to Hitnatkut: The Impact of Gush Emunim and the Settlement Movement on Israeli Politics and Society," 197.

land. But Gush Emunim perceives '*hitnachalut*' as a positive term. "Hitnachalut was the term used in the Bible to describe Joshua's conquest of the Land following the return from Egyptian exile. Unlike the rest of Israeli society, which distinguishes between the self ascribed positive notion of 'hityashvut' (settlement) as contrasted with the negative notion of 'hitnachalut' (squatting)."[96]

All in all Gush Emunim is an extreme right-wing movement, but only partly national-religious. Idith Zerdal/Akiva Eldar summarize this in the following way: "Judaism, Zionism, settlement, security, sacrifice, and redemption – the main pillars of the Zionist project in the Land of Israel and its ethos – were the motors that drove Gush Emunim."[97] Today Gush Emunim is not as influential as it was in its early phase in the late 1970s and early 1980s.

3. The Habad movement and its Approach to Settlement Policy

Unlike Gush Emunim, the Habad movement was not involved in the establishment of settlements. As seen in all arguments discussed, Habad is very concerned about the *bonne condition* of the Jewish people. Indeed, the approach to assure a secure life of Jews differs in comparison to Gush Emunim, the messianic thinking is of a rather different nature, as "only the miraculous Redeemer ... can bring Israel [the people] out of exile; the Jews are commanded only to prepare their hearts."[98]

The Habad movement has never regarded the State of Israel as holy, nor has it regarded the Land of Israel as a place (*makom*) where *galut* ends before the coming of redemption. Only the Messiah can bring the diaspora to an end, until then the diaspora reigns on the whole earth. In spite of all skepticism toward the Land of Israel, *Eretz Yisrael*, and the State of Israel, the Habad movement has always had strong ties to *Eretz ha-Kodesh* (the Holy Land, as the Land of Israel is called), long before the advent of secular Zionism.[99] The State of Israel cannot be seen as a legitimate Jewish state, if

---

[96] Ibid., 207.

[97] Eldar and Zertal, *Lords of the Land - The War Over Israel's Settlements in the Occupied Territories, 1967 - 2007*: 184.

[98] Aviezer Ravitz☐y, "The Contemporary Lubavitch Hasidic Movement - Between Conservatism and Messianism," in *Accounting For Fundamentalisms - The Dynamic Character of Movements*, ed. R. Scott Appleby and Martin E. Marty (Chicago, London: The University of Chicago Press, 1994), 318.

[99] Cf Ehrlich, *The Messiah of Brooklyn - Understanding Lubavitch Hasidism Past and Present*: 111.

it is reigned by non-religious Jews, therefore the State can never have any connections to the 'inception of Redemption,' not only because of its secularity, but also because it was never envisaged a Jewish state before the actual appearance of redemption.[100] "Habad does not support the 'negation of Galut' approach. While the members of Habad, like other [ultra-]orthodox Jews, perceive Galut as a negative form of existence, they do not share the total rejection of Diaspora culture and way of life, and they oppose the opinion that there is no more place for Jewish existence in the Galut."[101]

For Habad it does not matter where you live.[102] Immigration to Israel is not relevant – the Yiddish newspaper *Allgemeiner Journal*, a quasi-official organ of Habad, proclaimed: "The Lubavitcher rebbe clarifies that genuine [Jewish] life is possible especially if one lives and works in Exile."[103] It is no wonder that the headquarters of the Habad movement is located in 770 Crown Heights in New York and not in, for instance, Kfar Habad in Israel or directly in Jerusalem. The messianic section of Habad believes that the Messiah will come soon; the birth pangs took place with the Shoa and a few global events, the victory in the Six Day War, the breakdown of the Soviet Regime, and the First Gulf War[104], which were by the world Jewry

---

[100] Cf Friedman, "Habad as Messianic Fundamentalism - From Local Particularism to Universal Jewish Mission," 352.

[101] Don-Yehiya, "Two Movements of Messianic Awakening and Their Attitude to Halacha, Nationalism, and Democracy: The Cases of Habad and Gush Emunim," 276-77.

[102] "The dispersion of Jews in various countries worldwide ... is in external view a descent, and as much as the dispersion is greater, the descent is lower. ... 'It was God's grace that the Jews were dispersed among the nations.' The inner (=mystical) interpretation of this is well known: Wherever Jews arrive, they adopt the manners of the place ... But these customs later are used to serve religious purposes, and thus are elevated to become a part of the worship of God. ... Through this dispersion they gained a higher degree of the Worship of God, the merit of redeeming the Sparks [of holiness] that dwell in the customs of *all* countries and *all* places. [Emphasis in original.]" Benjamin Brown, "Rabbi Menahem Mendl Schneersohn of Lubavitch," in *The Blackwell Reader in Judaism*, ed. Jacob Neusner and Alan J. Avery-Peck (Cornwall: Blackwell Publishers Ltd, 2001), 252.

[103] Friedman, "Habad as Messianic Fundamentalism - From Local Particularism to Universal Jewish Mission," 345.

[104] *The Rebbe* claimed that the Israeli Jewry, mainly his local disciples, would be protected by G-d. The gas masks distributed by the IDF were refused by the Habadniks. In contrast, *the Rebbe* saw this war as the prelude to the Time of Redemption: "The time of your redemption has arrived." Cf Ravitz☐y, "The Contemporary Lubavitch

regarded as relevant. These may be signs for the end of times before *the* End of Times, and the beginning of *geulah* with the arrival of Messiah, who then will lead all Jews to Israel.[105] But where the Jews may have resided before is irrelevant, in contrast the younger R. Kook who claimed: "To be a Jew today, one must first and foremost live in Israel. ... Each Jew who comes to Israel, every tree that is planted in the ground of Israel, every rifle that is added to the Israeli army represents another real spiritual stage, another step toward redemption."[106]

The following proposal by *the Rebbe* may serve as a counter-argument: "Even in the land of Israel it is possible to be in the situation and the condition of 'slaves,' and furthermore, the exile in the land of Israel through the wicked of Israel is much worse than the exile outside the land through the wicked of the nations of the world."[107] *The Rebbe* wanted to say that in contrast to the claim that the land of Israel is the so-called paradise for Jews, it may be even worse due to wars with Arabs and the international condemnation of Israel. However, to reside in the United States, for instance, does not have to be as bad as to live in Israel, as there are no wars in this country and, notwithstanding the obvious advantages for *the Rebbe*, it would not be possible to have *yehidut* (conversations) with the Sixth Rebbe Yosef Yitzchak Schneerson, the *frierdiker Rebbe* (former Rebbe), who died in 1950, at his grave. Furthermore, one always has to bear in mind the mission of the Habad movement to 'disperse the springs,'[108] as already proclaimed by the *Besht* – the Messiah will only come if every Jew on the whole earth knows about the Habad movement's *Weltanschauung*.

A deeper understanding of the *Besht's* phrase is possible. A Jew lives in *galut* outside of the geographic borders of the State of Israel, if the point is true that the Land of Israel is already holy; nonetheless the Jew is no more enslaved by the world, as he would be, if he felt free in the land of Israel.

Hasidic Movement - Between Conservatism and Messianism," 315. And cf Don-Yehiya, "Two Movements of Messianic Awakening and Their Attitude to Halacha, Nationalism, and Democracy: The Cases of Habad and Gush Emunim," 289.

[105] Cf Don-Yehiya, "Two Movements of Messianic Awakening and Their Attitude to Halacha, Nationalism, and Democracy: The Cases of Habad and Gush Emunim," 279.

[106] Citation taken from ibid., 280.

[107] Citation taken from Wolfson, *Open Secret - Postmessianic Messianism and the Mystical Revision of Menahem Mendel Schneerson*: 133.

[108] Cf Friedman, "Habad as Messianic Fundamentalism - From Local Particularism to Universal Jewish Mission," 347.

This has to be understood as a mystical reference, because the third Rebbe stated: "And you know that the land of Israel is the disclosure of divinity [*gilluy elohut*] by means of involvement with the Torah and worship of the heart."[109]

To further delve into this discussion, one has to know that *the Rebbe*, Menachem Mendel Schneerson, knew of a significant difference in the Hebrew word *ha-olam*. One the one hand *ha-olam* is the Hebrew word for *world*, and on the hand the same word is read as *he'lem*, this means *concealment* or *hiddenness*.

At the moment the world is confronted with holiness being concealed as a consequence of human transgressions. But, eventually, this matter will be rectified when the spiritual essence of the corporeal will be manifested in the corporeal essence of the spiritual, "in terms of the belief that the land of Israel, which is holy, will spread forth in all lands, and then 'it will be revealed to every eye that the whole of the world in its entirety, which was created by means of the ten sayings, is holy.'" Therefore, it does not matter where you reside; for the moment nothing is holy as we are living in a world of transgression, but when the Messiah will come, then there will be no world of transgression anymore, and then nothing is unholy, because the Land of Israel will spread to every place on the planet.[110] It is now easier to derive from these statements that the State of Israel is not seen as holy or given any special religious consideration by the Habad movement – Israel is only a place like any other place on earth.

Though, there is a non-insignificant attachment to this argument which must not be dropped. *The seventh Rebbe* proclaimed in the beginning of his leadership as Rebbe that the interiority of the Torah in combination with the revealed aspect of the Torah should be "in the manner that they become one reality in actuality ... for by means of the study of Hasidism the desire is augmented, and through this also the understanding and comprehension of study of the revealed."[111] This is for importance to *the Rebbe Schneerson*: "Even the interiority of the Torah that will be disclosed in the future was already bestowed in the giving of the Torah."[112] The imparting of the Torah was a one-time event. This is of significance because we are confronted

---

[109] Citation taken from Wolfson, *Open Secret - Postmessianic Messianism and the Mystical Revision of Menahem Mendel Schneerson*: 132.

[110] Cf ibid.

[111] Citation taken from ibid., 172.

[112] Citation taken from ibid., 171.

with two matters of the Torah, the exoteric, the obvious and known, and the esoteric, the mystic meaning of the Torah. According to *the Rebbe*, the dedication to both dimensions has to be prepared in order to disclose the messianic Torah (*gilluy torato shel mashiah*).

"The revelation of the essence in the future comes about through the worship (avodah) of the Jew during exile [*galut*] – in the form of Torah study and commitment to ritual practice, which facilitates the 'breaking and nullification of the concealment ... that is from the manifold darkness.'"[113] The esoteric part can only be understood in reference to the exoteric part thus making the hidden dimension accessible enabling one to reach *dvekut*, since G-d and Torah are one essence.

Keeping this in mind, we will take a look at the argument of R. Shneur Zalman that "the commandments will not be nullified in the messianic future, but they will be purified in the aspect of the interiority of the Torah that will be revealed at that time, to the point that ritual observance will bring about the knowledge (da'at) through which one is 'comprised in the light of the Infinite.' (nikhlal be-or ein sof)."[114] Therefore, settlement of the occupied territories purifies the country, which *the Rebbe* benignly concedes or demands, under the condition that the Israeli government has Jews settle there to build Habad *yeshivot*. The *frierdiker Rebbe* had already proclaimed with explicit religious intentions in mind: "With God's help, we have great power, and we have to be active and to engage in all things necessary [for bringing about redemption] ... as this is the will of God that we will act and He will help us."[115]

It has to be understood that only the inner purification of every single Habadnik in the respective settlements will lead to the purification of the occupied territories. A Habadnik, as it has been taught since the establishment of Hasidism, has to reach *dvekut*, or better a kind of mystical experience, in which one leaves his body and reaches higher areas, the total self-abnegation – *bitul*. It may already be enough to lead a life in which Habadniks meticulously oblige the Commandments. This includes especially, as will be discussed below, to love one's neighbor,[116] thus the Palestinians.

---

[113] Ibid., 173.

[114] Ibid., 174.

[115] Citation taken from Don-Yehiya, "Two Movements of Messianic Awakening and Their Attitude to Halacha, Nationalism, and Democracy: The Cases of Habad and Gush Emunim," 275.

[116] Cf Loewenthal, *Communicating the Infinite - The Emergence of Habad School*: 10.

In other words, the Habadnik comes close to G-d. This gives the man a power or an awareness descending to earth and imparting a special power, by which the world is affected (thus it is transformed, purified, and even healed of all its maladies[117]).[118] This, in turn, is a step toward the elevation of the land of Israel or the Greater Land of Israel, from the lowest point to a higher region. This consequently leads to a future, in which "the land of Israel will spread to all lands." And this purification will enter "all of the synagogues and houses of study in all of the world ... in the true and perfect redemption by our righteous Messiah, the leader of the generation, for he is the Messiah of the generation."[119] Hence, the corporeal is eschatologically elevated surpassing the spiritual. The corporeal is the land or place (*makom*),[120] the land of Israel, which spreads all over the world.

Reviewing these points, the messianic argument is ambiguous and paradox in the way the *theo-ideology* of the Habad movement constructs it. It proclaims, on the one hand, that it does not matter where you live, because *galut* is in fact on everywhere on earth. It will only end when the End of Times and coming of the Messiah is reached. On the other hand, this is combined with the other part of the Habad's argument: it is a religious obligation to settle the occupied territories to purify the land to hasten the redemption. This means that you actively hasten the redemption by settling the territories, whereas, at the same time, it does not matter where you reside, because you are not allowed to actively hasten it, wherefore you have to be passive; and *Eretz Ha-Kodesh* is not any holier than any other place on earth. The fact remains, that the Habad movement promotes settlement building, but it does not enforce it through an organization.

Therefore the Habad movement can be considered to be extremely rightwing. They opposed, for instance, the Peace treaty with Egypt.[121] But they

---

[117] This may be done, according to Baal Shem Tov, only by a Zaddik. But today, it may be possibly done by many persons with a proper understanding of the Habadic meaning of the Torah. Cf ibid., 16, 20.

[118] Cf ibid., 7.

[119] Citations taken from Wolfson, *Open Secret - Postmessianic Messianism and the Mystical Revision of Menahem Mendel Schneerson*: 134.

[120] Cf ibid.

[121] "The Rebbe opposed Israel's territorial concessions in the Camp David agreement [of 1979] as misguided. After stressing the highly unstable political climate of Arab countries like Egypt, he warned: 'With whom can Israel sign a valid peace treaty now? With no one! Those who cry for 'peace' and 'peace now' deliberately choose to ignore such points. ... They are ready to make concessions which will place the lives

did not oppose it out of the same intentions as Gush Emunim. Gush Emunim actively opposed the settlement withdrawal, but Habad only took position against it, because of a danger for Jewish lives (*nefesh pikuach*). Furthermore, the reaction to the Oslo Accords was different to Gush Emunim's: "Much of our [the Habad movement's] concern for Israel is motivated by apprehension over the fate of the Jews there."[122] Eliyahu Touger, a Habadnik, who adapted texts of *the Rebbe* in a very polemical writing, claims that their highest intention is to save Jewish souls. As discussed above, the majority of Gush Emunim hates Arabs and kills them if they want to. Unlike Habad that asks: "What is the course of action that will protect Jewish and for that matter, Arab lives most effectively?"[123] Touger explains that Jews are ranked first, because the Torah teaches Jews "to place Jewish life as the highest priority," though all humans are created "'in the image of G-d,' and every life must be cherished."[124] The Habad movement, Touger advocates, wants to keep the occupied territories regardless of international pressure and the Palestinians' rights, as the state of Israel has to be more concerned about the lives of its own citizens and not about foreigners and non-Jews. Further Arabs are still mainly ruled by dictators. "The Arab regimes are for the most part totalitarian dictatorships prone to coups and unpredictable changes of heart."[125] But, Touger continues, the Palestinians' claim that the Jews stole their land is not legitimate and territorial concessions are not in harmony with the Halakhah.[126]

"What is our claim to the land? G-d's promise in the Torah. G-d told Abraham: 'I have given this land to your descendants.' For one-and-a-half thousand years the Land of Israel was our home, and ever since then, Jews

---

of millions of Jews in mortal danger." Hoffman, *Despite All Odds - The Story of Lubavitch*: 165.

[122] Eliyahu Touger, "Eyes Upon The Land - The Territorial Integrity of Israel - A Life Threatening Concern: Publisher's Foreword," Chabad, http://www.chabad.org/library/article_cdo/aid/72558/jewish/Publishers-Foreword.htm#footnoteRef1a72558. [06/03/2012].

[123] Eliyahu Touger, "Eyes Upon the Land - the Territorial Integrity of Israel - a Life Threatening Concern - Part 1 - The Principles Underlying The Israel-Arab Conflict," Chabad, http://www.chabad.org/library/article_cdo/aid/72559/jewish/Part-1.htm. [06/03/2012].

[124] Ibid. [06/04/2012].

[125] Ibid. [06/04/2012].

[126] Cf Don-Yehiya, "Two Movements of Messianic Awakening and Their Attitude to Halacha, Nationalism, and Democracy: The Cases of Habad and Gush Emunim," 290.

everywhere have longed to come home to their eternal heritage to Jerusalem, the site of the Holy Temple; to Hebron, the burial place of Abraham, Issac and Jacob; and to Bethlehem, where Rachel weeps for her dispersed children and awaits their return. Even throughout the two thousand years during which our people wandered from country to country, Israel has remained the national home of every Jew. From the beginning of the exile until this day, no matter how farflung his current host country might be, every Jew has turned to face the Holy Land in his thrice-daily prayers."[127]

In consequence of Touger's appeal, Habad wants to keep the occupied territories, because of G-d's help to get this land. "After thousands of years of exile, our people have returned to our land. Every portion of the land over which Jewish authority is exercised was won in defensive wars in which G-d showed overt miracles. Now when G-d grants His people land in such ways, should it be returned? Is it proper to spurn a Divine gift?"[128] G-ds presents are rare and must be treated accordingly.

Therefore, settlements have to be built, regardless of the Arabs of whom the Israelis do not have to take care, as there is much empty space. "The most immediate step to solving the problem is to settle the entire land. Wherever there is open space in Judea, Samaria, Gaza, and the Golan, settlements should be established. There is no need to displace Arabs; there is ample empty land."[129] This is a different approach as demanded by Gush Emunim, Touger continues in his settlement plans proposed to the Habad movement.

"This should not be done with fanfare. The idea is not to create an image, but to create a reality. When the land is settled by Jews, it will become obvious to all that we consider this as Jewish land, not theoretically, but practically. Indeed, the fact that settlement is the issue which the Arabs protest most vehemently should make it clear that it is Israel's highest priority. It is the most pragmatic means at Israel's disposal to change the balance of power in her favor. Once widespread settlement becomes a fact, it will impossible to turn back the clock. The Arabs outside Israel will appreciate that the borders will not be moved back. And the Arabs inside Israel will understand that their future exists in coexistence with the Jews and not with struggle against them."

---

[127] Touger, "Eyes Upon the Land - the Territorial Integrity of Israel - a Life Threatening Concern - Part 1 - The Principles Underlying The Israel-Arab Conflict". [06/04/2012].
[128] Ibid. [06/04/2012].
[129] Ibid. [06/04/2012].

According to my opinion, this paragraph shows a certain naivety, which reminds one of the novel *Altneuland* by Theodor Herzl, in which Arabs and Jews live together in utopian peace. Furthermore, the way to establish hard facts by building settlements must be questioned, although Touger highlights in his essay that the international community and the Arab states have no right to interfere with Israel. The question remains, however, for whom Touger produces facts. He does not mention it, but one can derive the messianic intention of a purification of the occupied territories.

It is to be assumed that Arabs will not appreciate Israel's settlement policy, as Touger emphasizes in his essay: "Whoever wants a clear picture of whether or not the Arabs desire peace should ask the ordinary Arab in the street. He will respond ... that he is not opposed to violence against Israel, and that he desires Arab dominion over the entire land of Palestine. ... The Arab world's attitude toward Israel is one of hatred and contempt; never have there been any serious attempts towards coexistence."[130] At least, Touger does not go too far by demanding that the occupied territories should be settled and the Arabs displaced. In contrast to Gush Emunim, he thinks that Arabs and Jews can coexist in peace. Touger, however, does not answer the question hovering over most of his essay: How shall Arabs and Israelis live together in peace, if their claims on land clash?

Touger substantiates his arguments with references to *the Rebbe*. "The Rebbe called for settlement of the entire land, emphasizing that not only from a spiritual perspective, but also from a security perspective, the Land of Israel is a single, indivisible entity. He did not see the government's program of partial settlement as a solution, for it placed the settlers in danger, and never reflected a sincere commitment to command authority over the land in its entirety."[131] Touger also refers to important spiritual and esoteric intentions and does not solely rely on security issues.

The reason for the concessions Israel is willing to make to the Habadniks is clearly based on the bible phrase: "We were like grasshoppers in our eyes, and so we were in their eyes!"[132] This was Moses' scouts' impression, who sent this message to him, having reached the Promised Land. Touger assumes that Israel and all Jews see themselves as 'puny' and this is the

---

[130] Ibid. [06/04/2012].

[131] Eliyahu Touger, "Eyes Upon The Land - Part 2 - Phases in the Israel-Arab Conflict - Israeli Approaches and Suggested Alternatives," Chabad, http://www.chabad.org/library/article_cdo/aid/72563/jewish/Part-2.htm. [06/04/2012].

[132] Numbers 13:33. Stone and Stone, *Tanach - The Stone Edition*.

reason why their enemies, who adopt this point of view, are so aggressive, wherefore the State of Israel made concessions on land.[133] If Jews had more self-respect, without 'boastful pride,' then other nations would regard them differently.[134]

The above mentioned concessions have, according to a reference by *the Rebbe*, a big disadvantage: it would increase terrorism.

"As the autonomy [of the Palestinian National Authority, for the establishment of the Oslo Accords] expands, the Jewish settlements within its territory are becoming vulnerable islands surrounded on all sides by hostile armed forces. In a sudden mass attack (which in Eastern Europe used to be called a pogrom) just before Purim, 1996, in the yeshiva building at the Tomb of Joseph in Shechem (Nablus), fifteen soldiers were killed and sixty other Jews were wounded by arms which Israel has handed to the Palestinian Autonomy's 'police force' as part of the 'peace process' ... Speaking with obvious pain, the Rebbe stated clearly that concessions would increase terrorist activity, rather than discourage it. 'The concessions convince the Arabs of Israeli weakness,' he emphasized. 'They make it clear that terrorism is effective in achieving results. Even mere talk of possible concessions is harmful because it encourages terrorist activity.'"[135]

Finally, the question remains why Habad is so concerned about the well-being of a state they do not regard as holy – only as holy in a mystical way, but which is for the moment of no further importance to it. The answer is Jewish unity as Touger claims in harmony with Jewish monism, seen from a standpoint of Habad theology:[136]

"We are all involved. Every Jew is bound to every other Jew: a threat to a Jewish community in any part of the world affects Jews all over the world.

---

[133] "Time and time again, the Israelis have buckled under pressure. Even when all the cards where in their hand, they have given in to Arab demands. Take, for example, the Camp David agreements [of 1978]: Carter needed a treaty for his election campaign. Sadat needed a treaty to put himself in the American camp. He had already burnt all his bridges behind him. Who had the strongest position? Begin. And yet he gave in to all the Arab demands." Touger, "Eyes Upon the Land - the Territorial Integrity of Israel - a Life Threatening Concern - Part 1 - The Principles Underlying The Israel-Arab Conflict". [06/04/2012].

[134] Cf ibid. [06/04/2012].

[135] Touger, "Eyes Upon The Land - Part 2 - Phases in the Israel-Arab Conflict - Israeli Approaches and Suggested Alternatives". [06/04/2012].

[136] Cf Ravitz☐y, "The Contemporary Lubavitch Hasidic Movement - Between Conservatism and Messianism," 311.

How much more so is this true when the Land of Israel is involved. *For every Jew, wherever he lives, possesses a portion in the Land of Israel. And the Land of Israel possesses a portion of every Jew, a piece of our heart and soul.* [Emphasis in original.]"[137]

In spite of all the presumable suspicions against Arabs that they are not trustworthy ("For the Arabs have broken every treaty they ever made with Israel."[138]), that they only want all of Palestine ("The Arabs will always claim that they have a valid goal: reclaiming a land that is rightfully theirs."[139]), and that they will drive the Jews into the sea ("The Jewish community inside and outside Israel sincerely believed the Arab threats to push Israel into the sea."[140]), Touger believes:

"The Palestinians are tired of losing their sons and their daughters; they are frustrated by the fact that they haven't been able to work freely and advance themselves financially for the last decade. ... They will focus their attention on their own lives and the options that are open to them. .. And hopefully, these advances [of Israel making no concessions anymore and being firm against the world pressures and the Arabs] will include the dawning of the age in which 'nation will not lift up sword against nation, nor will they learn war any more.'"[141]

In conclusion, Touger thinks that peace for both sides, the Jews and the Arabs, as he simplifies them, would be the best solution. Touger does not talk about the displacement of Arabs to Israeli neighbor states, as was often proclaimed by Gush Emunim. Yanki Tauber agrees with him concerning this point:

"Don't they see that *every time* they make concessions to their enemies, or even *talk* about making concessions – *more people die*? More Jews die, and more Arabs die, and the sufferings of both peoples increase. Yet when they hold firm, refuse to give up any land, and fight the killers with intelligence and determination, there are fewer Jewish casualties, fewer Arab deaths, and the lives of both peoples improve. [Emphasis in original.]"[142]

---

[137] Touger, "Eyes Upon the Land - the Territorial Integrity of Israel - a Life Threatening Concern - Part 1 - The Principles Underlying The Israel-Arab Conflict". [06/04/2012].

[138] Ibid. [06/04/2012].

[139] Ibid. [06/04/2012].

[140] Touger, "Eyes Upon The Land - Part 2 - Phases in the Israel-Arab Conflict - Israeli Approaches and Suggested Alternatives". [06/08/2012].

[141] Ibid. [06/04/2012].

[142] Tauber, "Land for Peace?". [06/04/2012].

One aspect clearly crops up again and again in the course of the discussion: Habad is only passive in settlements, but Habad supports it actively.[143] They just claim that Israel is not important as it is also *galut*, but they are worried about the lives of every Jew and every human being, therefore settlements should be built; and Habad also takes into consideration the purification of the Land for the hastening of the redemption.

It has to be added that the Habadniks are concerned about the Holy Land, since they claim that the Holy Land is in every Jew as the Jew is in the Holy Land. This is the reason for *the Rebbe* to take a firm stand and a rightist position: the neighbor states of Israel may endanger the lives of Jews; therefore it is not advisable to return land to the neighbors.[144] *The Rebbe* is only in favor of settlements for the safety of Jews, if the aforementioned are endowed with 'institutions of Torah,' as this purifies the country and brings about a lasting peace. Though *the Rebbe* took no active position in favor of settlements, he still claimed one could 'settle all the territories.'[145]

In review, in contrast to the active position of Gush Emunim, the Habad movement radically supports settlements, but due to a number of various reasons. First of all, as it is obvious for Habad, settlements in occupied territories secure peace for Israel, as the Jewish settlers live together with Palestinians in harmony. Jewish lives are not as endangered as they would be, if a hostile Arab state were erected in the West Bank.

Secondly, the purification of the Greater Land of Israel would bring an elevation to it by cleansing the land of its impure being. Though this does not mean that any Arab should be expelled, but only that the land became impure by an absence of Jews and it should be pure to hasten redemption, in a passive way by supporting settlements, but not by being actively involved in this policy.

---

[143] Cf Ehrlich, *The Messiah of Brooklyn - Understanding Lubavitch Hasidism Past and Present*: 104.

[144] "At the beginning of 1992, for example, the Rebbe demanded that the government of Israel stand firm against any international pressure and refuse to grant autonomy to the Palestinian inhabitants of the West Bank and Gaza Strip. In his words, political or civil autonomy would likely bring about, over the course of years, the establishment of an independent, hostile Palestinian state." Ravitz□y, "The Contemporary Lubavitch Hasidic Movement - Between Conservatism and Messianism," 320.

[145] Cf Heilman and Friedman, *The Rebbe - The Life and Afterlife of Menachem Mendel Schneerson*: 212.

All in all the settlement policy of the Habad movement has been paradox from its beginning on. *The Rebbe* supported it as much as he negated it, he supported it to save Jewish souls, he negated it as he saw Israel as a unit and not as a negation of *galut*. The reason for a messianic future was a factor for the Habad movement to support the construction of new settlements in the occupied areas.

Chapter IV: Conclusion

The care for the well-being of Jews and Messianic anticipation were the main characteristics for the Habad movement throughout the paper.

I began in the first chapter by giving a definition of the ultra-Orthodox Jews, which is according to my opinion the best that fits for an ultra-Orthodox Jew or Haredi. All the historical descriptions I gave did not explain the actual interest of the Habad movement in Israel, but they highlighted important issues to understand the next chapters. The first chapter has to be seen as an introduction to the circumstances Israel and the Haredi society are in today.

The second chapter, thus, did away with the enigma; as I covered the difficulties to give the final definition of whom the State of Israel, the supposed Jewish State, lets immigrate and whom not under the application of their *Law of Return*. And I went to explain, that R. Jacob Immanuel Schochet made it clear in his pamphlet, which was written for the reason to have an impact on the State of Israel, that the Habad movement did care about the every single case which happened in the long history of the state, but the Habad movement does care more about the definition of a Jew. A Jew can only be a Jew, if she/he is one according to the Halakhah. The Halakhic laws set the basis and then one can discuss who does fit to it, but not the other way around. The same case applies for the converts, here Schochet thumped much more on the Halakhah that not only Israel does not accept non-Orthodox conversions, but that it is better if there will not be any unhalakhic converts anymore, especially not made by reform or conservative Jews, who all deviate from the Halakhah. The messianic importance may be seen in the unity of all Jewish souls; thus any 'Jew,' who is not a real Jew, as she/he did not convert in a halakhic way, is a danger for the Jewish entity. The Messiah will not come, if individual Jews of the Jewish entity are not able to fulfill spiritual journeys.

The next argument about the Six Day War was based more on *nefesh pikuach* – the care for Jewish souls, while the war happened and afterwards. The war was primarily won through the prayer with *tefillin* which produced the G-dly connection *en masse*, according to Habad. The territories Israel gained have to be kept to secure Israel herself. Furthermore, I discussed the question why redemption will come soon – even if directly after the Six Day War only victory was claimed by the Habad movement to have been brought about by them and no messianic meaning was given to the territories, later though this victory was seen as a global phenomenon which, in its view, may be a sign for the soon coming of the Messiah.

In the last chapter I discussed the extreme right-wing and now more or less obsolete Gush Emunim, which was established in 1974, at the beginning of the building of settlements in the occupied territories, and gained much success, but after the death of its spiritual mind R. Kook Jr. and after the accomplishment of many settlements in the West Bank the decline of the bloc began. The bloc was very active and violent in the construction of settlements. They not only fought their declared enemy, the Arabs, but also the IDF, but notwithstanding all this there were also some persons in the bloc who were more on the dovish side.

In contrast, the Habad movement was passive. It called for settlements to save Jewish souls. *Nefesh pikuach* illustrates again and again to be the main intention for the current condition of Jews by the movement. Habad did not engage in active settlement construction. Nonetheless, in their mind the movement had not to care about the land as it does not matter where you live – everywhere is *galut* (exile). But some messianic breeze was to be felt, as *the Rebbe* proclaimed that the purification of the gained territories will be a positive step toward redemption.

All in all, the paper showed the intentions of the Habad movement to participate in Israeli politics, that they are based on the Jewish *raison d'être* to save foremost Jews, but nonetheless to save all human beings – in reality. And there has always been a messianic element in the arguments as well, even if Israel is not more important than any other place on the earth. The Habad movement, however, demands a purification of the land for redemption (*geulah*). Furthermore, the Habadniks are concerned in which the way Jews are Jews. In the *Weltanschauung* of the Habad movement, it is better if more people become orthodox Jews or, even better, Habadniks, as only a Jewish entity is able to introduce *geulah*.

The paper also represented in very clear terms, in the examples, the difficulties one faces, when trying to analyze the thinking and political interest of the movement, not only of the movement's paradoxes, but also because of its sometimes contradictory ways.

The paper made it clear to me why the Habad movement, as an ultra-Orthodox movement with its anti-Zionistic tendencies, takes so much interest in Israel. In the future, it is likely that the Habad movement remains without a new leader, but will continue to influence Israeli politics as it has always done before – maybe the movement will even be willing to take on more responsibility in the State of Israel.

Chapter V: Glossary

Agudat – organization/party
Alter Rebbe – First Rabbi
Alufo shel Olam – the Ruler of the World
Aliyah – immigration to Israel
Am Yisrael – the Israeli People
Apikursut – heresy
Avodah - worship
Avodah zarah – idolatry
Ayin – Naught
B'ikvata d'mesihah – brought by the Messiah
Besht – Baal Shem Tov (Master of the Good Name)
Beit Din – court
Binah – understanding
Bitul – selfabnegation
Daat – knowledge
Dayan/dayanim – judge/-s
Derechei Hasidut – Hasidic way (pious way)
Din rodef – license to kill a fellow Jew
Dvekut – communion with G-d
Ein Sof – the Infinite
Eretz - land
Eretz Yisrael – Israel
Eretz ha-Kodesh – the Holy Land
Erlicher yidn – pious Jews
Frierdiker Rebbe – former Rebbe
Galut – exile, diaspora
Gaon – genius
Geulah – redemption
Gilluy elohut – disclosure of divinity
Goy/goyim – non-Jew/s; non-Jewish nation
Halakhah – Jewish law
He'lem – hiddenness, concealment
Ha-olam – the world/earth
Haredim/Haredi/Haredic/Haredism – ultra-Orthodox Jews/Jew/ultra-Orthodoxism

Hasidim/Hasidut – pious people/pious

Haskalah – Jewish Enlightenment

Hesder – special national-religious unit in the IDF

Heteirim – relaxations of restrictions

Hiloni/m – secular Jew/s

Hitnachalut – conquest, squatting

Hitnatkut – disengagement

Hityashvut - settlement

Hokhmah – wisdom

Hokhmah Ilaah (Chochmah Ilaah) – supernal wisdom

Humrot – stringent interpretations of commandments

Huz laaretz – outside of the State of Israel

Kabbalat ol mitzvot – acceptance of the yoke of the commandments

Kehilla/Kehillot – Jewish community/-ies

Kol Elohi – Divine All

Likutei Amarim – collection of statements

Lituani/Lituanim – Lithuanian/s (name for Mitnaggdim today)

Makom/ha-makom – place

Malkhut Yisrael – the kingdom of Israel

Merkaz Harav – Center of the Rabbi (yeshiva of the R. Kooks, national religious yeshiva)

Mikveh – ritual bath

Mila - circumcision

Mitnaggdim – opponents

Mitteler Rebbe – the in-between rabbi

Mitzvah/mitzvoth – commandment/s

Moshiach - Messiah

Musar - ethics

Nefesh – soul; mind

Nefesh bahamit/nefeshim bahamitot – animal soul/s

Nefesh elokhit – g-dly soul

Nefesh pikuach – care of a Jewish soul

Neshamah – soul; spirit; life

Or Ein Sof – Light of the Infinite

Oleh/olim – immigrant/-s

Payot – sidelocks

Qulot – lenient interpretation of commandments

Rebbe/Rebbeinim – rabbi/rabbis

Ruach – spirit; intellect

Sefer/Seforim – Holy Book/Books
Sfira/sfirot – vessel/vessels
Shechitah – ritual slaughter
Shekhinah – the female part of G-d/last vessel
of the ten sfirot in Kabbalah
Shila/shilot – emissary/-ies
Shulchan Aruch – Jewish Code of Law
Tanya – teachings outside of the Mishnah
Taryag mitzvoth – 613 commandments
Tefillin – phylacteries
Tevila – full body immersion in a ritual bath (mikveh)
Tomchei Temimim – Supporters of the pure ones
(first Yeshiva of Habad)
Torah Lishmah – study of Torah for its own sake
Torah shelo lishmah – study of Torah not for its own sake
Trefe medina – unkosher state
Yehidut – conversations with the Rebbe
Yesh – Material World
Yeshiva – Talmud school
Yidishkeit - Jewishness
Yiras shomayim – fear of Heaven
Zaddik – Righteous person
Zimzum – contraction; veiling

Chapter IV: Bibliography

Agudat-Israel. "Zum Programm Der Agudas Jisroel." Translated by J. Hessing. In *The Jew in the Modern World - a Documentary History*, edited by Paul R. Mendes-Flohr and Jehuda Reinharz. New York, Oxford: Oxford University Press, 1980.

Alfassa, Shelomo. "Lubavitch's Break-Away Religion of 'Schneersonism' Is Growing." Shelomo Alfassa, http://alfassa.com/schneersonism.html.

Angel, Marc D. "Torah Can Be Used to Let New Jews in, Not Keep Them Out." Haaretz, http://www.haaretz.com/opinion/torah-can-be-used-to-let-new-jews-in-not-keep-them-out-1.432080.

Arens, Moshe. "It's Wrong to Push out Israeli Settlers, Even If Its Legal." Haaretz, http://www.haaretz.com/opinion/it-s-wrong-to-push-out-israeli-settlers-even-if-its-legal-1.427420.

Bar-Lev, Mordecai. "Tradition and Innovation in Jewish Religious Education in Israel." Chap. 4 In *Tradition, Innovation, Conflict - Jewishness and Judaism in Contemporary Israel*, edited by Benjamin Beit-Hallahmi and Zvi Sobel. 101-31. Albany: State University of New York, 1991.

Baumel, Simeon D. "Weekly Torah Portions, Languages, and Culture among Israeli Haredim." *Jewish Social Studies* 10, no. 2 (2004): 153-78.

Beit-Hallahmi, Benjamin, and Zvi Sobel. "Introduction." Chap. 1 In *Traditon, Innovation, Conflict - Jewishness and Judaism in Contemporary Israel*, edited by Benjamin Beit-Hallahmi and Zvi Sobel. 1-22. Albany: State University of New York, 1991.

Ben-Rafael, Eliezer. *Jewish Identities - Fifty Intelllectuals Answer Ben Gurion* [in Hebrew]. Kiryat Sede-Boqer: Ham Merkaz Le Moreset Ben Gurion, 2001.

Beyer, Lisa. "Expecting the Messiah." The Rick Ross Institute Internet Archives, http://www.rickross.com/reference/lubavitch/lubavitch18.html.

Biale, David. "Gershom Scholem on Jewish Messianism." Chap. 21 In *Essential Papers on Messianic Movements and Personalities in Jewish History*, edited by Marc Saperstein. Essential Papers on Jewish Studies, 521-50. New York, London: New York University Press, 1992.

Blaha, Charles O. "U.S. Strongly Objects to Hrc's Creation of One-Sided Fact Finding Mission on Israeli Settlements." Permanent Mission of the United States of America in Geneva, http://geneva.usmission.gov/2012/03/22/israeli-settlements/.

Braunold, Joel. "What Is a 'Jewish State'?" Haaretz, http://www.ha-aretz.com/jewish-world/what-is-a-jewish-state-1.415908.

Brown, Benjamin. "Orthodox Judaism." Chap. 18 In *The Blackwell Companion to Judaism*, edited by Jacob Neusner and Alan J. Avery-Peck. Blackwell Companions to Religion, 311-33. Oxford: Blackwell Publishers Ltd, 2000.

— — —. "Rabbi A. Y. Kook on Ideological Diversity and Unity." In *The Blackwell Reader in Judaism*, edited by Jacob Neusner and Alan J. Avery-Peck. Cornwall: Blackwall Publishers Ltd, 2001.

— — —. "Rabbi Menahem Mendl Schneersohn of Lubavitch." In *The Blackwell Reader in Judaism*, edited by Jacob Neusner and Alan J. Avery-Peck. Cornwall: Blackwell Publishers Ltd, 2001.

Carroll, Robert, and Stephen Pricket, eds. *The Bible - Authorized King James Version with Apocrypha*. Oxford, New York: Oxford University Press, 1997.

Dan, Joseph. *Die Kabbala - Eine Kleine Einführung*. Translated by Christian Wiese. Ditzingen: Reclam, 2007.

Deutsch, Nathaniel. "The Forbidden Fork, the Cell Phone Holocaust, and Other Haredi Encounters with Technology." *Contemporary Jewry* 29, no. 1 (2009): 3-19.

Dinur, Benzion. "The Origins of Hasidism and Its Social and Messianic Foundations." Chap. 4 In *Essential Papers on Hasidism - Origins to Present*, edited by Gershon David Hundert. Essential Papers on Jewish Studies, 86-208. New York, London: The New York University Press, 1991.

Don-Yehiya, Eliezer. "The Book and the Sword - the Nationalist Yeshivot and Political Radicalism in Israel." Chap. 11 In *Accounting for Fundamentalisms - the Dynamic Character of Movements*, edited by R. Scott Appleby and Martin E. Marty. 264-302. Chicago, London: The University of Chicago Press, 1994.

— — —. "Traditionalist Strands." Chap. 7 In *Modern Judaism: An Oxford Guide*, edited by Nicholas Robert Michael De. Lange and Miri Freud-Kandel. 93-105. Oxford, New York: Oxford University Press, 2005.

— — —. "Two Movements of Messianic Awakening and Their Attitude to Halacha, Nationalism, and Democracy: The Cases of Habad and Gush Emunim." Chap. 7 In *Tolerance, Dissent, and Democracy - Philosophical, Historical, and Halakhic Perspectives*, edited by Moshe Sokol. 261-309. Northvale: Jason Aronson Inc., 2002.

Dor, Elad, and Nati Tucker. "Arabs, Haredim Not Working Will Become Macro Danger." The Marker.com, http://english.themarker.com/arabs-haredim-not-working-will-become-macro-danger-1.323886.

Dowty, Alan. *The Jewish State - a Century Later*. Berkeley, Los Angeles, London: University of California Press, 1998.

Ehrlich, Mark Avrum. *Leadership in the Habad Movement - a Critical Evaluation of Habad Leadership, History, and Succession - with Particular Emphasis on Menachem Mendel Schneerson*. Northvale: Aronson, 2000.

— — —. *The Messiah of Brooklyn - Understanding Lubavitch Hasidism Past and Present*. Jersey City: KTAV Publishing House, 2004.

Eldar, Akiva, and Nir Hasson. "Jerusalem Mayor Aims to Establish New Settlement in East Jerusalem." Haaretz, http://www.haaretz.com/news-/national/jerusalem-mayor-aims-to-establish-new-settlement-in-east-jerusalem-1.422228.

Eldar, Akiva, and Idith Zertal. *Lords of the Land - the War over Israel's Settlements in the Occupied Territories, 1967 - 2007*. New York: Nation Books, 2007.

Elior, Rachel. "Habad - the Contemplative Ascent to God." Chap. 6 In *Jewish Spiritualiy - from the Sixteenth Century Revival to the Present*, edited by Arthur Green. World Spirituality - an Encyclopedic History of the Religious Quest, 157-205. London: Routledge & Kegan Paul, 1987.

— — —. *The Mystical Origins of Hasidism*. Translated by Shalom Carmi. Oregon: The Littmann Library of Jewish Civilization, 1999.

— — —. *The Paradoxical Ascent to God - the Kabbalistic Theosophy of Habad Hasidism*. Translated by Jeffrey M. Green. Albany: State University of New York, 1993.

Etkes, Immanuel. *The Besht - Magician, Mystic, and Leader*. Translated by Saadya Sternberg. Hanover, London: University Press of New England, 2005.

— — —. *The Gaon of Vilna - the Man and His Image*. Translated by Jeffrey M. Green. Berkely, Los Angeles: University of California Press, 2002.

— — —. *Rabbi Israel Salanter and the Mussar Movement - Seeking the Torah of Truth*. Translated by Jonathan Chipman. Philadelphia: Jewish Publication Society, 1993.

Ettinger, Yair. "Hundreds of Ultra-Orthodox Jews Protest in Jerusalem against 'Exclusion of Haredim'." Haaretz.com, http://www.haaretz.-com/news/national/hundreds-of-ultra-orthodox-jews-protest-in-jerusalem-against-exclusion-of-haredim-1.404783.

― ― ―. "Israel Interior Ministry Still Letting Chief Rabbinate Decide 'Who Is a Jew'" Haaretz, http://www.haaretz.com/print-edition/-news/israel-interior-ministry-still-letting-chief-rabbinate-decide-who-is-a-jew-1.402198.

Fischer, Karsten. "Fundamentalismus." In *Politische Theorie Und Politische Philosophie - Ein Handbuch*, edited by Martin Hartmann and Claus Offe. 192-94. München: C.H. Beck, 2011.

Freeman, Tzvi. "Tradition or Progress." Chabad, http://www.-chabad.org/library/article_cdo/aid/269549/jewish/Tradition-or-Progress.htm.

Friedman, Menachem. "Habad as Messianic Fundamentalism - from Local Particularism to Universal Jewish Mission." Chap. 13 In *Accounting for Fundamentalisms - the Dynamic Character of Movements*, edited by Martin E. Marty and R. Scott Appleby. 328-57. Chicago, London: The University of Chicago Press, 1994.

― ― ―. "Life Tradition and Book Tradition in the Development of Ultraorthodox Judaism." Chap. 7 In *Judaism Viewed from within and from Without*, edited by Harvey E. Goldberg. 235-55. Albany: State University of New York Press, 1987.

Goldberg, Giora, and Efraim Ben-Zadok. "Gush Emunim in the West Bank." *Middle Eastern Studies* 22, no. 1 (1986): 52-73.

Goldschmidt, Henry. "Religion, Reductionism, and the Godly Soul: Lubavitch Hasidic Jewishness and the Limits of Classificatory Thought." *Journal of the American Academy of Religion* 77, no. 3 (2009): 547-72.

Haaretz-Editorial. "Netanyahu Did the Right Thing by Clearing Hebron Outpost." Haaretz, http://www.haaretz.com/opinion/netanyahu-did-the-right-thing-by-clearing-hebron-outpost-1.422668.

― ― ―. "Ulpana Can't Turn into a Memorial for Israel's Rule of Law." Haaretz, http://www.haaretz.com/opinion/ulpana-can-t-turn-into-a-memorial-for-israel-s-rule-of-law-1.427041.

― ― ―. "Un Probe Must Take West Bank out of Israeli Hands." Haaretz, http://www.haaretz.com/opinion/un-probe-must-take-west-bank-out-of-israeli-hands-1.421844.

Hareuveni, Eyal. *By Hook and by Crook - Israeli Settlement Policy in the West Bank*. Translated by Zvi Shulman. edited by Yael Stein B'tselem.org: B'tselem, 2010.

Hausen, E. "Gericht: Abriss Illegaler Siedlungsgebäude Bis Anfang Juli." Israelnetz.com, http://www.israelnetz.com/themen/innenpolitik/artikel-innenpolitik/datum/2012/05/08/gericht-abriss-illegaler-siedlungsgebaeu-de-bis-anfang-juli/.

Heilman, Samuel C. *Defenders of the Faith - inside Ultra-Orthodox Jewry*. Berkley, Los Angeles, London: University of California Press, 1992.

Heilman, Samuel C., and Menachem Friedman. *The Rebbe - the Life and Afterlife of Menachem Mendel Schneerson*. Princeton, NJ [u.a.]: Princeton Univ. Press, 2010.

— — —. "Religious Fundamentalism and Religious Jews - the Case of Haredim." Chap. 4 In *Fundamentalisms Observed*, edited by Martin E. Marty and R. Scott Appleby. The Fundamentalism Project, 197-263. Chicago: The University of Chicago Press, 1991.

Heilman, Samuel C., and Fred Skolnik. "Haredim." In *Encyclopaedia Judaica*, edited by Michael Berenbaum and Fred Skolnik. Detroit: Macmilan, 2007.

Hoffman, Edward. *Despite All Odds - the Story of Lubavitch*. New York: Simon and Schuster, 1991.

IDF-Spokesman. "Evacuation of Israeli Civilians from the Gaza Strip Completed." Ministry of Foreign Affairs, http://www.mfa.gov.il/MFA-/Government/Communiques/2005/Evacuation+of+Israeli+civilians+from+the+Gaza+Strip+completed+22-Aug-2005.htm.

Israeli-Government. "Law of Return." Israel Ministry of Foreign Affairs, http://www.mfa.gov.il/MFA/MFAArchive/1950_1959/Law+of+Return+5710-1950.htm.

JPost.com-Staff. "Barak: Consider 'Hilltop Youth' a Terror Group." Jerusalem Post, http://www.jpost.com/Defense/Article.aspx?id=249390.

Kaplan, Eran. "Israeli Jewry." Chap. 11 In *Modern Judaism: An Oxford Guide*, edited by N.R.M.D. Lange and Miri Freud-Kandel. 144-54. Oxford, New York: Oxford University Press, 2005.

Katz, Jakob. "Towards a Biography of the Hatam Sofer." Translated by David Ellenson. Chap. 10 In *From East and West - Jews in a Changing Europe, 1750 - 1870*, edited by Francis Malino and David Sorkin. 223-66. London: Blackwell Publishing, 1990.

— — —. *Tradition and Crisis - Jewish Society at the End of the Middle Ages*. New York: Schocken Books, 1974.

Kershner, Isabel. "Israeli Girl, 8, at Center of Tension over Religious Extremism." The New York Times, http://www.nytimes.com/2011/12/28/-world/middleeast/israeli-girl-at-center-of-tension-over-religious-extrem-ism.html?_r=1&sq=ultra%20orthodox%20israel&st=cse&scp=2&pagewan-ted=all.

Landau, David. *Piety and Power - the World of Jewish Fundamentalism*. New York: Hill and Wang, 1993.

Laqueur, Walter. *A History of Zionism - from the French Revolution to the Establishment of the State of Israel*. New York: Schocken Books, 2003.

Leshno-Yaar, Aharon. "Statement to the Unhrc by Israel's Ambassador Aharon Leshno-Yaar." Israel Ministry of Foreign Affairs, http://www.mfa.gov.il/MFA/Foreign+Relations/Israel+and+the+UN/Issues/Response_UNHRC_commission_settlements_22-Mar-2012.

Levinson, Chaim. "Idf Demolishes Third Illegal West Bank Outpost This Week." Haaretz, http://www.haaretz.com/news/national/idf-demolishes-third-illegal-west-bank-outpost-this-week-1.406870.

— — —. "Ulpana Developer Lied and Told Residents That Outpost Was Built on Wzo, Not Palestinian Land." Haaretz, http://www.haaretz.com/news/diplomacy-defense/ulpana-developer-lied-and-told-residents-that-outpost-was-built-on-wzo-not-palestinian-land-1.430640.

Lis, Jonathan, and Natasha Mozgovaya. "Netanyahu: It Is Israel's Right and Obligation to Build in Jerusalem." Haaretz, http://www.haaretz.com/news/diplomacy-defense/netanyahu-it-is-israel-s-right-and-obligation-to-build-in-jerusalem-1.393341.

Loewenthal, Naftali. *Communicating the Infinite - the Emergence of Habad School*. Chicago: The University of Chicago Press, 1990.

Mackey, Robert. "The Israeli Tv Report on Gender Segregation That Sparked Protest." In *The Lede*, edited by The New York Times, 2011.

Maimonides. *Mishneh Torah - the Book of Knowledge*. Translated by Moses Hyamson. Jerusalem: Boys Town Jerusalem Publishers, 1965.

Mindel, Nissan. *The Divine Commandments*. 11th ed. New York: Kehot Publication Society, 1945.

Morris, Benny. *Righteous Victims - a History of the Zionist-Arab Conflict, 1881 - 2001*. New York: Vintage Books, 2001.

Münch, Peter. "Gefahr Für Demokratie Und Sicherheit." Süddeutsche Zeitung, http://www.sueddeutsche.de/politik/gewalt-juedischer-siedler-gefahr-fuer-demokratie-und-sicherheit-1.1235272.

Netanyahu, Binyamin. "Speech by Pm Netanyahu to a Joint Meeting of the U.S. Congress." Israel Prime Minister's Office, http://www.pmo.gov.il/PMOEng/Communication/PMSpeaks/speechcongress240511.htm.

Newman, David. "From Hitnachalut to Hitnatkut: The Impact of Gush Emunim and the Settlement Movement on Israeli Politics and Society." *Israel Studies* 10, no. 3 (2005): 192-224.

Nowak, D. "Netanjahu Gegen Illegale Siedlungsaußenposten." Israelnetz, http://www.israelnetz.com/themen/innenpolitik/artikel-innenpolitik/datum/2011/11/08/netanjahu-gegen-illegale-siedlungsaussenposten/.

of Breslev, Rebbe Nachman. "Teffilin - the Skin of Imagination." Chabad.org, http://www.chabad.org/kabbalah/article_cdo/aid/380355/jewish/Tefillin-Skin-of-the-Imagination.htm.

of Lyady, R. Schneur Zalman. "Likutei Amarim - Chapter 19." Kehot Publication Society, http://www.chabad.org/library/tanya/tanya_cdo/aid/1028943/jewish/Chapter-19.htm.

— — —. "Likutei Amarim - Chapter 39." Kehot Publication Society, http://www.chabad.org/library/tanya/tanya_cdo/aid/1029067/jewish/Chapter-39.htm.

— — —. "Likutei Amarim Chapter 3." Kehot Publication Society, http://www.chabad.org/library/tanya/tanya_cdo/aid/1028876/jewish/Chapter-3.htm.

— — —. "Likutei Amarim Chapter 33." Kehut Publication Society, http://www.chabad.org/library/tanya/tanya_cdo/aid/7912/jewish/Chapter-33.htm.

— — —. "Likutei Amarim Chapter 35." Kehot Publication Society, http://www.chabad.org/library/tanya/tanya_cdo/aid/1029034/jewish/Chapter-35.htm.

— — —. "Likutei Amarim Chapter 37." Kehut Publication Society, http://www.chabad.org/library/tanya/tanya_cdo/aid/7916/jewish/Chapter-37.htm.

— — —. "Schulchan Aruch - Orach Chaim." 2000 Project Genesis, http://www.torah.org/advanced/shulchan-aruch/classes/orachchayim/chapter24.html.

— — —. "Tanya - Likutei Amarim, Chapter 2." Kehot Publication Society, http://www.chabad.org/library/tanya/tanya_cdo/aid/1028875/jewish/Chapter-2.htm.

— — —. "Tanya Likutei Amarim Chapter 37." Kehot Publication Society, http://www.chabad.org/library/tanya/tanya_cdo/aid/1029047/jewish/Chapter-37.htm.

Pfeffer, Anshel. "Jerusalem's Public Transport System as Metaphor for Israel in 2012." Haaretz.com, http://www.haaretz.com/print-edition/news/jerusalem-s-public-transport-system-as-metaphor-for-israel-in-2012-1.405732.

Plaut, Mordecai "Should Non-Jews 'Return' under the Law of Return?" Chareidi.org, http://www.chareidi.org/ATCOTU/snjrutlor.html.

Rabinovich, Itamar, and Jehuda Reinharz, eds. *Israel in the Middle East - Documents and Readings on Society, Politics, and Foreign Relations, Pre-1948 to the Present*. Second ed. London, Hanover: Brandeis University Press, 2008.

Rabinowicz, Harry M. *The World of Hasidism*. London: Vallentine, Mitchell, 1970.

The Encyclopedia of Hasidism. Northvale: Aronson, 1996.

Rader, Benzion. "Why Teffilin?" Chabad.org, http://www.chabad-.org/therebbe/article_cdo/aid/133500/jewish/Why-Tefillin.htm.

Ravid, Barak. "Israel Cuts Contact with Un Rights Council, to Protest Settlements Probe." Haaretz, http://www.haaretz.com/news/diplomacy-defense/israel-cuts-contact-with-un-rights-council-to-protest-settlements-probe-1.420786.

— — —. "U.S. Pressing Un Human Rights Commissioner to Put Off West Bank Settlements Probe." Haaretz, http://www.haaretz.com/blogs-/diplomania/u-s-pressing-un-human-rights-commissioner-to-put-off-west-bank-settlements-probe-1.427744.

Ravitzky, Aviezer. *Messianism, Zionism, and Jewish Religious Radicalism*. Chicago [u.a.]: Univ. of Chicago Press, 1996.

Ravitz⬚y, Aviezer. "The Contemporary Lubavitch Hasidic Movement - between Conservatism and Messianism." Chap. 12 In *Accounting for Fundamentalisms - the Dynamic Character of Movements*, edited by R. Scott Appleby and Martin E. Marty. 303-27. Chicago, London: The University of Chicago Press, 1994.

Rosenberg, Oz. "Hundreds of Ultra-Orthodox Protesters Riot in Flashpoint Town of Beit Shemesh." Haaretz.com, http://www.haaretz.com-/news/national/hundreds-of-ultra-orthodox-protesters-riot-in-flashpoint-town-of-beit-shemesh-1.404470.

Rosenberg, Shmarya. "Rabbi David Berger - Shmuley Boteach 'Wrong'." Shmarya Rosenberg, http://failedmessiah.typepad.com/failed_messiah-com/2008/01/rabbi-david-ber.html.

Schneerson, Rebbe Menachem Mendel. *About the Question: Who Is a Jew and About Converts in a Halakhic Commentary* [in Hebrew].

— — —. "Exile+1 = Redemption." http://www.chabad.org/library/-moshiach/article_cdo/aid/1192683/jewish/Exile-1-Redemption.htm.

— — —. "The Rebbe Speaks to Hillel Students." Chabad, http:/-/www.chabad.org/therebbe/article_cdo/aid/392177/jewish/The-Rebbe-Speaks-to-Hillel-Students.htm.

Schneerson, Rebbe Yosef Yitzchak. "Chassidic Discourses - Chapter Iv." Kehot Publication Society, http://www.chabad.org/library/article_cdo/aid/73656/jewish/Chapter-IV.htm.

Schochet, Elijah Judah. *The Hasidic Movement and the Gaon of Vilna.* Northvale: Aronson 1994.

Schochet, R. Jacob Immanuel. "Who Is a Jew? 30 Questions and Answers About This Controversial and Divisive Issue." http://www.whoisajew.com/.

Scholem, Gershom. "Devekut, or Communion with God." Chap. 8 In *Essential Papers on Hasidism - Origins to Present*, edited by Gershon David Hundert. Essential Papers on Jewish Studies, 275-98. New York, London: New York University Press, 1991.

Scholem, Gershom "Die Jüdische Mystik in Ihren Hauptströmungen." Sinzheim: Suhrkamp Taschenbuch Verlag, 1967.

Sheshkin, Ira M., and Arnold Dashefsky. "Jewish Population in the United States 2011." North American Jewish Data Bank, http://www.jewishdatabank.org/Reports/Jewish_Population_in_the_United_States_2011.pdf.

Silber, Michael K. "The Emergence of Ultra-Orthodoxy - the Invention of a Tradition." Chap. 2 In *The Uses of Tradition - Jewish Continuity in the Modern Era*, edited by Jack Wertheimer. 22-84. New York: Jewish Theol. Seminary of America u.a., 1992.

Sinclair, Daniel. "Halakhah and Israel." Chap. 28 In *Modern Judaism - an Oxford Guide*, edited by Miri Freud-Kandel and Nicholas Robert Michael De. Lange. 352-62. Oxford, New York: Oxford University Press, 2008.

Sprinzak, Ehud. *The Ascendence of Israel's Radical Right*. New York: Oxford University Press, 1991.

Stadler, Nurit. *Yeshiva Fundamentalism*. New York, London: New York University Press, 2009.

Stengel, Richard. "Bibi's Choice." *Time* 179, no. 21 (28 May, 2012 2012).

Stone, Irving, and Helen Stone, eds. *Tanach - the Stone Edition*. edited by Rabbi Nosson Scherman. New York, Bnei Brak: Mesorah Publications, 2000.

Tauber, Yanki. "Land for Peace?" Chabad.org, http://www.chabad.org/library/article_cdo/aid/82019/jewish/Land-for-Peace.htm.

— — —. "What Makes a Jew 'Jewish'?" Chabad.org, http://www.chabad.org/library/article_cdo/aid/45132/jewish/What-Makes-a-Jew-Jewish.htm.

Touger, Eliyahu. "Eyes Upon the Land - Part 2 - Phases in the Israel-Arab Conflict - Israeli Approaches and Suggested Alternatives." Chabad, http://www.chabad.org/library/article_cdo/aid/72563/jewish/Part-2.htm.

— — —. "Eyes Upon the Land - the Territorial Integrity of Israel - a Life Threatening Concern - Part 1 - the Principles Underlying the Israel-Arab Conflict." Chabad, http://www.chabad.org/library/article_cdo/aid/72-559/jewish/Part-1.htm.

— — —. "Eyes Upon the Land - the Territorial Integrity of Israel - a Life Threatening Concern: Publisher's Foreword." Chabad, http://www.chabad.org/library/article_cdo/aid/72558/jewish/Publishers-Foreword.htm#footnoteRef1a72558.

unknown. "1974: The Mitzvah Tank." Chabad-Lubavitch Media Center, http://www.chabad.org/therebbe/timeline_cdo/aid/62178/jewish/1974-The-Mitzvah-Tank.htm.

— — —. "The Basics." Moshiach Campaign, Chabad.org, http://www.chabad.org/library/moshiach/article_cdo/aid/1157488/jewish/The-Basics.htm.

— — —. "Belief and Anticipation - the Basics." Moshiach Campaign, Chabad.org, http://www.chabad.org/library/moshiach/article_cdo/aid/1-121885/jewish/The-Basics.htm.

— — —. "The Conversion Crisis 1995 - Present." Anti Defamation League, http://www.adl.org/israel/conversion/crisis.asp#4.

— — —. "The Law of Return - Implementation Cases." Jewish Agency, http://www.jewishagency.org/JewishAgency/English/Jewish+Education/Compelling+Content/Eye+on+Israel/Activities+and+Programming/Law+of+Return/7.+The+Law+of+Return++Implementation+Cases.htm.

— — —. "The Messiah of Judaism." Truthnet.org, http://www.truthnet.org/TheMessiah/4_Messiah_of_Judaism/.

— — —. "The Oswald Rufeisen / Brother Daniel Case Court Summations." Jewish Agency, http://www.jewishagency.org/JewishAgency/English/Jewish+Education/Compelling+Content/Eye+on+Israel/Activities+and+Programming/Law+of+Return/19.+THE+OSWALD+-RUFEISEN.htm.

— — —. "The Six Day War and Teffilin." Jewish Educational Media, http://www.chabad.org/multimedia/media_cdo/aid/397220/jewish/The-Six-Day-War-and-Tefillin.htm.

— — —. "Testing the Principals." Anti Defamation League, http://www.adl.org/israel/conversion/testing-principles.asp.

— — —. "Who Is Moshiach? - the Basics." Moshiach 101, http://www.chabad.org/library/moshiach/article_cdo/aid/1121893/jewish/The-Basics.htm.

unknown, dpa, and AFP. "Ultraorthodoxe Juden Vergleichen Israel Mit Nazi-Reich." Zeit Online, http://www.zeit.de/politik/ausland/2012-01/-ultraorthodoxe-israel-protest.

— — —. "Ultraorthodoxe Randalieren in Beit Schemesch." Zeit Online, http://www.zeit.de/politik/ausland/2011-12/israel-ultra-orthodoxe.

Viorst, Milton. *What Shall I Do with This People? - Jews and the Fractious Politics of Judaism.* New York, London: The Free Press, 2002.

Walters, Neal. "Good Shabbos Everyone." Amerisoft Inc., http://www.amerisoftinc.com/wwwboard/messages/76.html.

Weill, Barbara. "Summary of Definitions on Who Is a Jew?" Jewish Agency for Israel, http://www.jafi.org.il/JewishAgency/English/Jewish+Education/Compelling+Content/Eye+on+Israel/Activities+and+Programming/Israel-Achieve/Summary+of+Definitions+on+Who+is+a+Jew.-htm.

Weissbrod, Lilly. "Gush Emunim Ideology — from Religious Doctrine to Political Action." *Middle Eastern Studies* 18, no. 3 (1982/07/01 1982): 265-75.

Wolfson, Eliot R. *Open Secret - Postmessianic Messianism and the Mystical Revision of Menahem Mendel Schneerson.* New York: Columbia University Press, 2009.